the **border** planner

First published in North America in 2000 by
Laurel Glen Publishing
An imprint of the Advantage Publishers Group
5880 Oberlin Drive, San Diego, CA 92121-4794
www.advantagebooksonline.com

Library of Congress Cataloging-in-Publication
Data

Bird, Richard.
      Border Planner/Richard Bird.
         p.cm
      ISBN 1-57145-675-9
      1. Garden Borders. 2. Gardens--Design.
      I. Title
SB424.B57 2000
635.9'63--dc21   00-032760

1 2 3 4 5   00 01 02 03 04
Produced by Toppan
Printed in China

Publishing Director Alison Goff
Creative Director Keith Martin
Executive Editor Julian Brown
Senior Designer Claire Harvey
Design Rima Design
Editor Karen O'Grady
Production Sarah Scanlon
Picture Research Liz Fowler

LG Publisher Allen Orso
LG Managing Editor JoAnn Padgett
LG Project Editor Elizabeth McNulty

the **border** planner

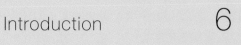

Introduction

The border is an essential building block of any garden, large or small. The way that borders are organized will greatly influence the appearance and character of a garden, and the plants that form its core are a vital part, transforming the garden from merely an outside space into an area of living beauty.

Borders are more than just a sum of their parts. They may have pleasing appearances as a whole, but when examined more closely the beauty of individual plants becomes apparent, adding another level of interest. And these plants in turn attract wildlife, which further enhances the garden.

The nature of borders and the plants they contain creates a wonderful atmosphere that acts as the perfect backdrop against which the owners and their friends can relax outside. They can be designed and laid out in such a way as to suit the mood and lifestyle of the gardener, in much the same way that the décor within the house provides a sympathetic environment.

Borders mean different things to different people. For some they are merely decoration, for others they are a way of filling empty space in the garden. However, there are many who really enjoy gardening and for them the border becomes a way of life. Many people who have no artistic pretensions find that planning and planting a border is a way to express themselves in color, while others just revel in the delights of being able to grow plants. Beyond the border, many find friendship and the ability to increase their knowledge through meeting other like-minded people, as one of the great joys of borders is to wander around them discussing the plants.

The sight of a large border burgeoning with flowers in full color can be daunting to someone who has never created one. However, they are not difficult to make; gardening is mainly common sense and the design has as much to do with personal preference as artistic ability. Nature is very forgiving and if things go wrong, you can always try something different the following year.

Nor do you need a great knowledge of plants before you set out to create your border; that will all come in time. Common, easy-to-grow plants can be used to create a border that is just as pleasing as one filled with unusual or rare varieties. Borders have to do with personal pleasure and should be created for the gardener, and perhaps his or her family, but no one beyond them. What the neighbors think is barely relevant, so fill it with plants that you enjoy. If they are common plants, or you do not have a clue as to what they are called, it does not matter.

Although creating a border is basically common sense and the design is up to you, there are certain guidelines that will help you on your way. This book sets out to provide advice on planning and planting a border from scratch to suit your own taste and lifestyle. It covers the more theoretical aspects, such as the use of color, as well as more practical details to put the theory into practice. It also provides plenty of inspiration with many different border styles and helps with the choice of suitable plants.

Border Planning

Planning is a vital part of the construction of any garden and the borders within it. Even seemingly random parts of the garden, such as wildlife areas or cottage gardens where everything may seem jumbled together, have a logic behind them, some form of fundamental philosophy. It is, therefore, important to look at the elements of design that go to make up a garden before attempting to create or make changes to one.

The basic idea is to create something you will enjoy, something that will give you pleasure. There is little point in creating borders that take up every second of your spare time and money simply to impress other people; if you lie in bed worrying about the state of your borders and what the neighbors think, it would be best to turn it all into lawn.

The first step is to decide what you want to create, what will give you pleasure. Draw up a list of desirable features such as whether you want to turn over the whole garden to borders, or whether you want some lawn or patio, or just paths in between the beds. What type of plants do you want to grow: sun lovers or shade lovers, for example, and what style of beds do you want to create: cottage-garden, romantic, formal?

Before you get down to the exciting task of designing these beds, you must take into account a few practical considerations. Will you have the time and energy to look after the beds, or will you have to compromise and have a smaller planted area simply because you will not be able to deal with larger ones? Can you afford to create what you want, or will it, again, be necessary to compromise? Are there other considerations that ought to be taken into account? For example, playing children and flower beds do not always mix well.
The answers to these questions will help you decide what type of border you want to create and how and where to do it.

Positioning a Border

The position of a border within a garden is very important, as it will not only dictate the appearance of the garden but also what you can grow in it. The best beginning is to have a blank canvas, an empty garden, where you can choose the position and shapes of your borders from scratch. Most gardeners are probably more likely to have an established garden, where perhaps there are existing borders that you want to take over, or there are other features such as mature trees, a greenhouse, or a pond that have to be taken into account when you are planning what you will do.

Sunny sites

Sunny borders are among the easiest to cope with, simply because there are so many plants that like to grow in an open, sunny position. The border can be in full sun for all of the day or perhaps lose it toward the end of long, summer days. There is a wide range of plants that grow in this position, including many with bright colors. Being in the sun and thus in the open, such borders are often not only dried by the sun but also by winds. It is therefore important to put as much well-rotted organic material as possible into the soil during the initial preparation and subsequently to treat it with a mulch at least twice a year.

In sunny positions, it is also possible to grow many plants that usually prefer shade, as long as there is plenty of moisture in the soil to keep the plants from drying out.

Below
Sun-loving plants are ideal for a raised bed in an open position with shelter from the wind.

Above
The cool colors of
shade-loving plants
are displayed in this
raised border.

Shade

Shade is often considered to be a real
problem from the gardener's point of view.
Nothing could be farther from the truth,
however, as long as one basic rule is
remembered: only grow plants in the shade
that grow in the shade in the wild. If you try to
grow sun-loving plants in the shade they will
fail, they will become drawn and miserable
and eventually die. On the other hand, if you
choose plants that naturally grow in
woodland or other shady conditions then you
will succeed. This means that you may have
to forgo many of the brighter bedding plants,
but you will discover a whole world of other
interesting and attractive species. In fact,
many gardeners create shade in their gardens
just so they can grow some of the wonderful
shade-loving plants available. A border in the
shade, therefore, can offer great scope. See
page 70 for additional details.

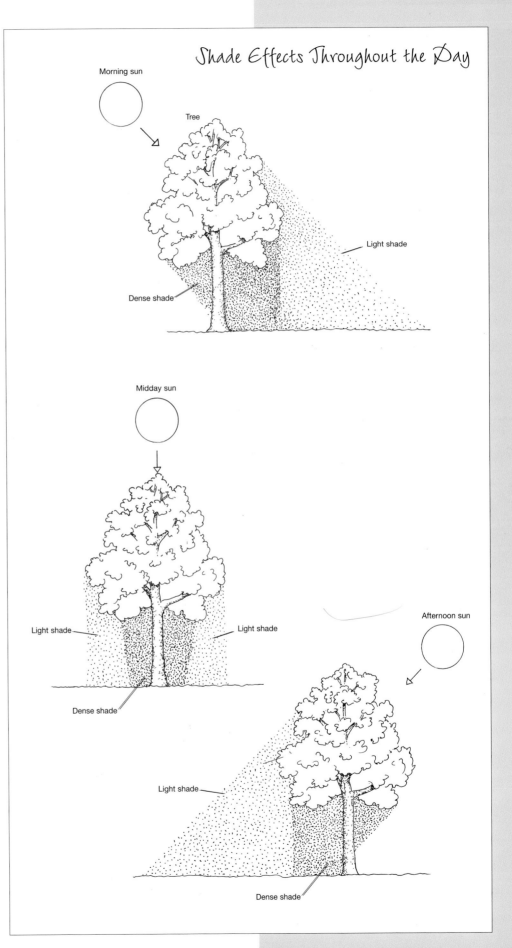

Shade Effects Throughout the Day

Morning sun

Tree

Light shade

Dense shade

Midday sun

Light shade

Light shade

Dense shade

Afternoon sun

Light shade

Dense shade

Sheltered or exposed sites

Another factor to consider when positioning a border is whether the site is sheltered or exposed to prevailing winds, and even frosts. An exposed site will limit the variety of plants you can grow: trees and shrubs will become misshapen, and softer plants, such as perennials, may simply blow over in very windy weather. This also affects the temperature: a sheltered border in a courtyard against the wall of a house will stay several degrees warmer than a border out in the garden, open to the elements. Bear this in mind when planning what to grow in a border and consider creating a windbreak—a hedge or fence, for example— if the area is very exposed.

Soil

Soil plays an important part in border planning. If the garden is in an area of alkaline soil, then it will be very difficult to grow plants such as heathers and rhododendrons, which will only grow on an acid soil. Similarly, an acid soil will preclude those plants that do better on an alkaline, or chalky, soil. It is possible to treat soils but this is not very satisfactory in the case of alkaline ones.

There is also the problem of areas with heavy soils. They are not very good for growing plants that require a free-draining soil, such as alpines. If you are keen to grow alpines and have heavy soil, ordinary borders will have to

Above
A sheltered border of hot colors including the arching stems of *Crocosmia* 'Lucifer.'

be avoided and raised beds built. Equally, sandy soils dry very quickly, making it difficult to grow plants such as hostas and other moisture lovers. However, there are many Mediterranean plants that like such conditions, and these are obviously the types of plants to choose.

Not only is there a question of location of the garden, but there is also the problem of different areas within it. Some areas of the garden may be drier than others, because of the slope of the land or large trees or shrubs removing moisture from the soil. Take this into account when deciding where to site your border, as the plants you wish to grow will be more suited to some areas of the garden than others.

Coping with existing features

Existing features will often dictate the position of a new border, or the plants that can be grown in an existing one. Trees, for example, can cast a dense shade and there is little point in trying to grow sun lovers under it. Choose woodland plants for such areas. More light can be admitted by trimming off some of the lower branches and this will also allow in more rain, thus increasing the number of plants you can grow successfully.

Tall buildings, walls, and fences can be a problem, even on the sunny side, as they are not only often dry at the base but also tend to reflect the wind back into the border, creating turmoil and breaking down plants. Also, tall plants will lean away in an attempt to get more light. So try to move the bed out a bit, away from the overhang. On the shady side of such obstacles it is best to grow woodlanders and other shade-loving plants. These positions are often short of water, so add plenty of moisture-retaining humus in the form of garden compost or farmyard manure to the soil. If permanently in shade, paint nearby walls or fences white if possible to reflect in more light.

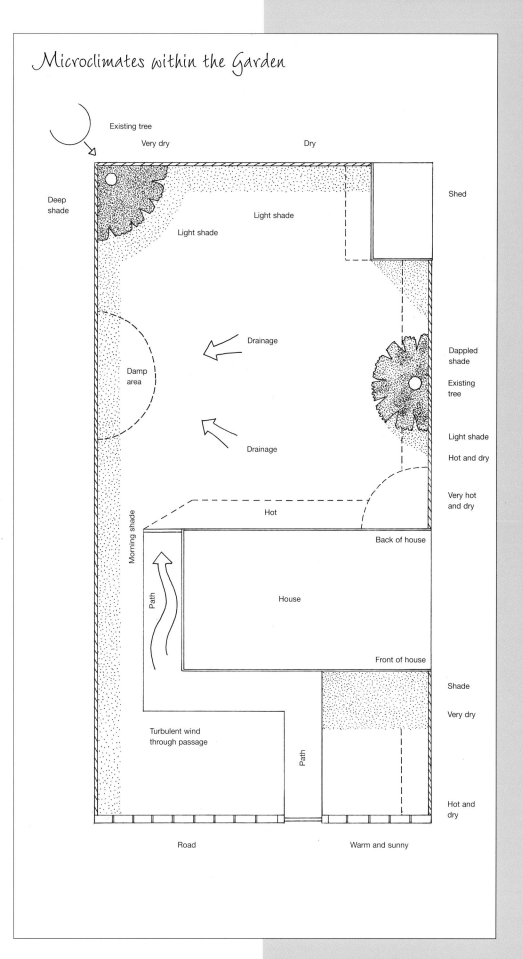

Microclimates within the Garden

Outlines and Border Shapes

The outline of a border is very important as it says a lot about the style you are creating. It will affect totally the mood and feeling of not only the border but also the garden as a whole. Straight lines and geometric shapes provide a formal setting, while sinuously curving borders bring a more informal feel to the garden.

Below

The informally arranged plants soften the straight lines of the brick framework.

Straight lines

Beds with straight lines tend to look rather formal. They require less fuss than curved edges, but tend to lack the interest of less formal designs, particularly as they reveal all at a glance, whereas curves disappear around corners. Straight-edged beds look particularly good where the arrangement of the plants is in a set pattern, to enhance the formality. If you are committed to straight lines but want a more informal image, then allow the plants to spread out over the boundaries, perhaps to flop over a path, for example, so that the straight line is broken and blurred.

Geometric shapes

Like straight lines, geometric shapes are more relevant to formal gardens and borders. A circular bed, for example, looks better filled with a formal bedding scheme than with informal hardy perennials. Avoid very sharp angles when planning borders, especially when making triangles and stars as these narrow points are very difficult to plant. Geometric borders are usually created for the effect of their shape, and filling them with large plants will often mask this. However, if they are used for low bedding schemes or if the outline is bordered with a low hedge, such as in a parterre or knot garden, then the shape will show.

Sinuous curves

Sinuous curves are much more interesting in most situations than straight lines. With the latter, the eye slips straight along the border to the end with nothing to arrest it. With curved borders, the eye stops at the next bend and has time to enjoy what is in the bed. This has the advantages of restricting the amount you can look at at any one time and providing an air of expectation of what lies just out of sight. As you walk along a curved border, more and more areas become visible, which before were hidden. However, the curves must be well thought out. Avoid drastic twists and turns as these tend to jar. A slow, shallow curve is much more pleasing to the eye.

Outlines and Border Shapes

The appearance of a garden can be changed dramatically by using curved or straight lines and features.

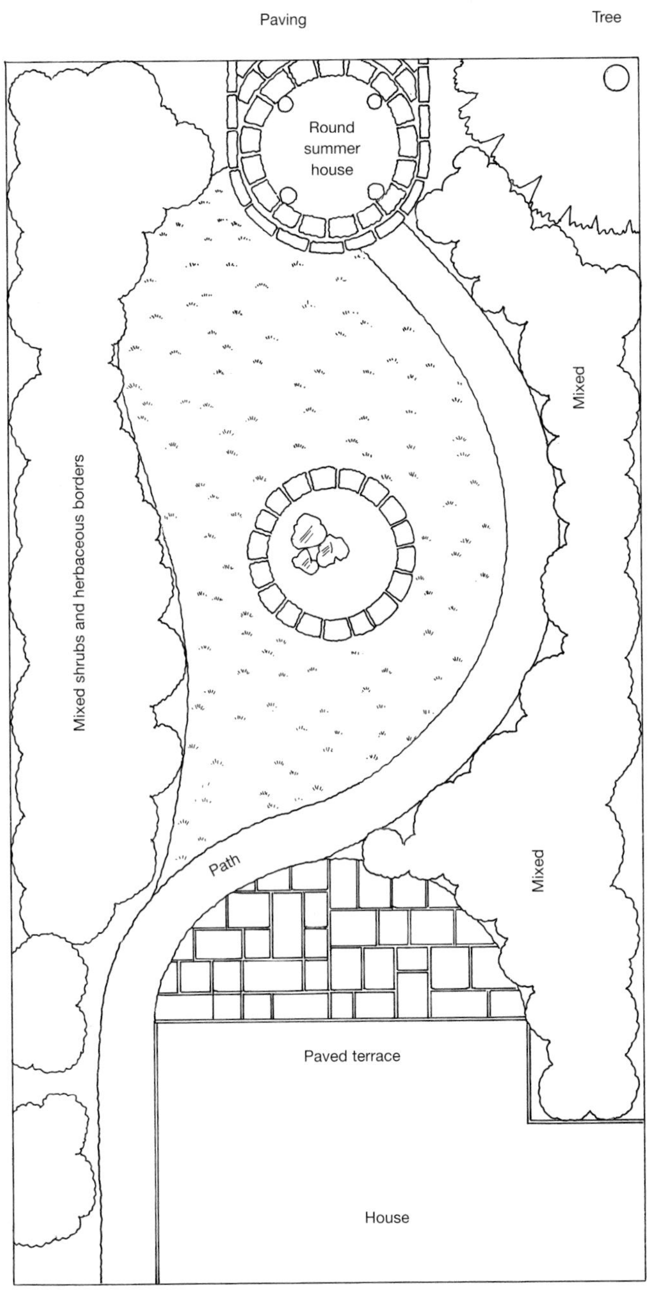

Paving

Tree

Round summer house

Tree

Mixed

Mixed

Mixed shrubs and herbaceous borders

Path

Paved terrace

House

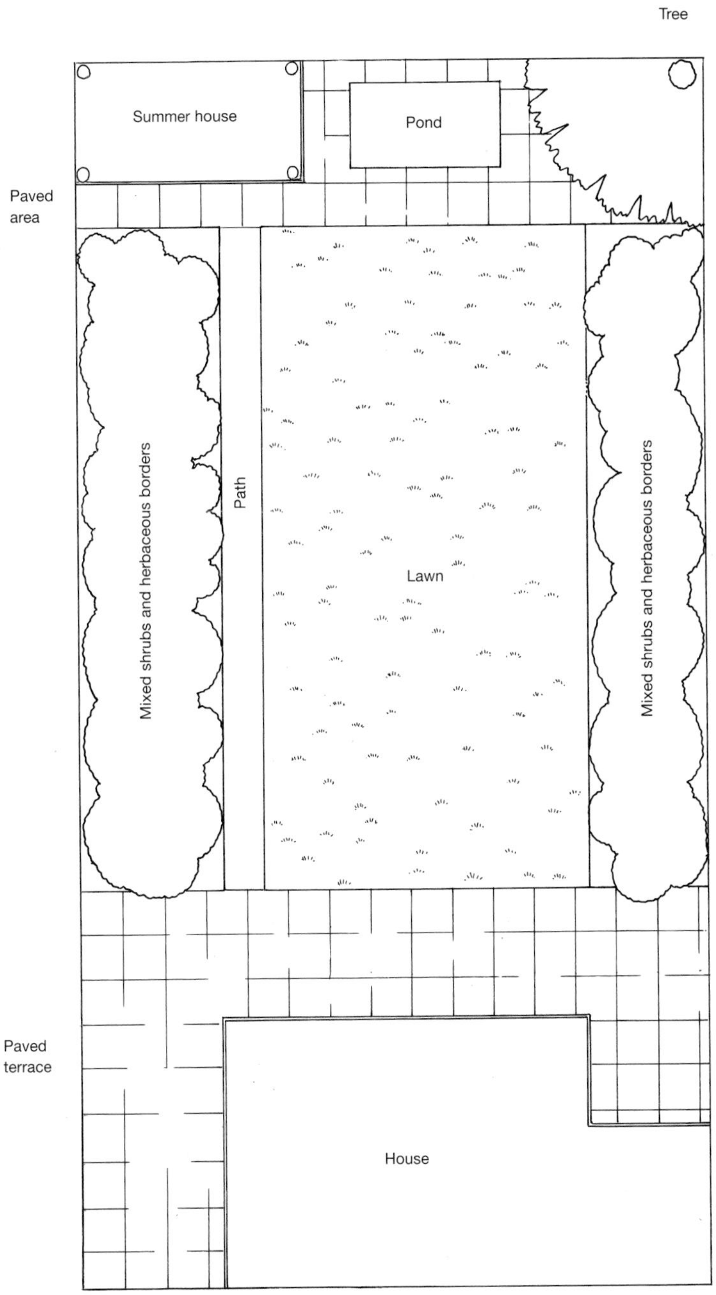

Summer house

Pond

Paved area

Mixed shrubs and herbaceous borders

Path

Mixed shrubs and herbaceous borders

Lawn

Paved terrace

House

Focal points

With a long, straight-edged border the eye is taken straight down the length of it to the end, revealing all as it goes. This is particularly true if there are two parallel borders with a path in between. This may not be a bad thing, as it can be rather impressive if the scale is large enough. It can also be useful if there is some form of focal point at the end of the path, perhaps a piece of sculpture, a stunning tree or a view into the landscape beyond. In this situation, the straight-edged borders will serve to highlight the focal point.

Maintenance

From a practical point of view, straight edges are the easiest to maintain. A line can be stretched along their length to act as a guide, or a length of wood can be placed along the edge, and the lawn or path trimmed to it. It is not so easy to use a guide on curved edges. Similarly, it is easier to mow along a straight edge than a curved one.

Left

This border of fuchsias curves away out of sight, creating the illusion that the garden may go on for a long way.

Below

The combination of height and sinuous curving line creates an illusion of greater depth.

Focal Points

A gate can act as a focal point drawing the eye rapidly toward it and giving the impression that the garden is longer than it is. Straight lines help the illusion.

The path seems to disappear around a corner, creating the illusion of a longer garden.

Backgrounds and Foregrounds

While some borders work in isolation, most must be considered in their context. The framework in which a border exists can affect its appearance dramatically. Herbaceous borders, for example, look dramatic when set against a tall hedge which acts as a plain backdrop, whereas this may be too overwhelming for a low border of bedding plants.

Island beds

Beds can be created without a background as such. These are island beds that are situated in the middle of lawns or paved areas. Unless these beds are large and it is therefore possible to grow tall plants in the middle, there is a tendency for the viewer either to look straight over the bed to what lies beyond or to be distracted by the fact that the border is too airy and has no substance. Island beds work best if there is an area of tall, dense plants in the center to act as a background to the surrounding planting, or if the plants are there as decoration rather than for individual appreciation. Such beds are ideal for bedding schemes, for example, where it is not the individual plants that count but the pattern they create.

Hedge backgrounds

A dark green hedge makes an ideal background for an herbaceous border. The plain expanse tends to bring out the colors and show up the plants in front. It also acts as a barrier, preventing the eye from traveling farther and keeping it within the area of the border. Unfortunately, hedges need cutting and their roots are hungry and thirsty, so it is a good thing to have a gap, such as a path, between the hedge and the border. This not only allows access to cut the hedge, but also

Below

This willow frame creates a rustic background to this border.

to the back of the border, something that can be difficult to reach in other circumstances without treading on close-packed plants. Yew (*Taxus baccata*) is one of the best hedging materials. Holly (*Ilex aquifolium*) is also a good hedging plant, but the fallen, spiny leaves can make weeding the border quite uncomfortable.

Walls and fences

Walls are also good for setting off plants as long as they are plain and simple. Concrete block walls with decorative holes are too fussy and detract from the border, as the eye is distracted by the pattern of the wall and the view through it. One big advantage of walls as opposed to hedges is that they can be used for a wide range of climbing plants, allowing vertical space for planting. Fences can also work, as long as they are solid. Again, decorative, open ones allow too many distractions. However, this can be offset by growing climbing plants against them. Wooden fences need to be treated with preservative, but do not use creosote as its fumes will kill many of the plants in the border.

Foregrounds

The foreground can also play an important role in the appearance of the border. A large stretch of grass, for example, is restful to the eye, and a garden with a central lawn area can appear more tranquil than one filled with borders. Grass also acts as a good foil for plants, but has the disadvantage that it needs regular mowing, and if the grass is not quite what it should be, weeds will often grow from it into the border, creating a lot of work.

Hard surfaces can also look attractive, especially if they are in natural colors, such as stone or earth-tone bricks. Some of the dyed paving slabs are not so successful, particularly if the colors are mixed, as they then compete with the colors in the border. Gravel is good, especially for paths. Chipped bark is also good for paths, but is best used in a woodland or shady situation, where it looks more natural than more formal hard surfaces.

Backgrounds and Foregrounds

A low planting in an island bed allows the eye to pass over it to more distant objects.

A higher planting in an island bed stops the eye and it is the bed that is observed rather than the distance.

How Much Work?

One of the problems of modern life is that we never have the time or energy to do all the things we want to do, no matter how much we like doing them. Gardening is one activity for which we often lack the time needed to do it properly. This is why it is vital to assess how much maintenance you will be able to manage, before planning and creating a border. This will allow you to tailor your borders, and the garden as a whole, to your lifestyle.

Below
A perfect ground cover of periwinkles, *Vinca major* 'Variegata' and bluebells, *Hyacinthoides hispancia.*

Low-maintenance borders

If you have little time for gardening but would like to grow a wide selection of plants, you will obviously have to plan a border containing plants that require little attention. All plants need some, however, especially if you want to keep the border looking good.

Trees are probably the most maintenance-free as they need little pruning. Unless you have a big garden it is not practical to have large woodland borders, but a few small trees such as ashes and birches can be included. Most shrubs need to be pruned if they are to perform at their best, but many gardeners just leave them alone, and although they may not flower as well, they still form attractive space fillers, with little attention required apart from planting them in the first place.

Perennials are a lot more labor intensive. Choose strong-growing forms that do not require staking, a big time-consumer. Also choose those with long seasons, that require little but being cut to the ground in autumn. Some of the hardy geraniums, such as *Geranium sanguineum*, are perfect for this. Those that depend on foliage for their attraction, such as hostas, ferns, and grasses, have a long season of interest.

Annuals are labor intensive if you grow your own. However, self-sown annuals need little attention apart from removing them when their task is done. Annual bedding will need deadheading from time to time, but considering the length of time it is in flower, it is a good value for the time spent.

Above
A dense area of heathers makes a good ground cover as long as the soil is thoroughly prepared beforehand.

Border preparation

One of the most time-consuming activities in the garden is weeding. It is also often the most hated. There are several ways of reducing the amount of work involved.

The first is to spend time preparing the ground as thoroughly as possible when creating the border in the first place. All perennial weeds should be removed because if any of these are left in the border they will reappear among the plants. Prepare the border during the autumn and then check it over in the spring before planting to remove any weeds that have reappeared.

Plant the plants reasonably close together so that once they are mature there is little or no bare earth showing. This will have the effect of reducing the light at soil level, making it more difficult for weed seedlings to establish and grow.

After planting, mulch the border with a layer of composted or chipped bark. This will help prevent weed seed from germinating. Other mulches can be used, such as gravel on an alpine or Mediterranean bed.

Watering

Watering is another time-consuming activity. In the well-prepared border, watering should not be necessary. Plenty of well-rotted organic material, such as garden compost or farmyard manure, should be added to the soil when it is dug. This will help to retain moisture down in the ground where it is required by the plant roots. Covering the soil with a mulch also helps by reducing the amount of evaporation. Composted or chipped bark is ideal for this.

Ground cover

A low-maintenance solution to planting a border is to use ground cover. Certain plants carpet the ground, helping to keep down the weeds and consequently the amount of work required. Some ground cover plants will look rather boring in a border, but any plants with plenty of foliage can be used as long as they are close enough together to exclude light from the ground. It is, however, very important to remember that ground cover will only suppress germinating seed; it will not kill existing perennial weeds, so these must all be removed before the ground cover is planted.

Below
A layer of bark chippings makes a good mulch as it is long-lasting and heavy enough not to blow away.

Acaena saccaticupula 'Blue Haze'
A low-growing perennial with handsome blue foliage and red flowers in summer

Anthemis punctata subsp. *cupaniana*
A low-growing perennial with silver foliage and white flowers in spring and early summer

Astrantia major
A perennial forming clumps of handsome, divided foliage with whitish-green flowers in summer

Bergenia cordifolia Elephant's ears
A perennial with round, evergreen leaves and pink or white flowers throughout the year

Epimedium rubrum
A perennial with evergreen foliage and red flowers in spring or early summer

Geranium macrorrhizum
A low-growing perennial with pink flowers in early summer

Hosta fortunei
A medium perennial with handsome foliage and summer flowers

Lysimachia nummularia 'Aurea'
A carpeting perennial with golden foliage and summer flowers

Pulmonaria angustifolia
A low-growing perennial with blue flowers in spring

Stachys byzantina Lamb's ears
A low-growing, silver-leaved perennial with pink flowers in summer

Thymus serpyllum Thyme
A carpeting shrub with evergreen leaves and pink, purple or white summer flowers

Vancouveria chrysantha
A low-growing perennial with yellow flowers in early summer

Planting a Border

Planting a border is the most creative aspect of gardening and, for this reason, many people shy away from the task. Yet very few aspects of our lives are not controlled by design or planning of one sort or another. When we get up in the morning we decide which clothes to wear. What is appropriate for what we are doing? Which shoes go with which dress, or which tie goes with which shirt? These are decisions that we all make all the time without stopping to think that we are considering design or color coordination; it is just something we do. To a varying degree we are all design literate in some ways. As with clothes, so with interiors. We all have opinions about what we like, what colors go with what, and how they should be mixed within a room or house.

And so it is in the garden. Without knowing it, most people have enough knowledge and experience drawn from their everyday lives to design a border, but because it is not something they do every day, or even every year, they often feel apprehensive and are uncertain of their abilities. There are one or two basic rules that act as guidelines, but these are mainly common sense. Most gardeners do follow them and, on the whole, the best gardens and borders conform to them, but rules are meant to be broken and if, for example, purple mixed with orange gives you pleasure, then use that combination in your planting schemes. Choose plants to fill your borders because you like them.

Having decided what it is practical to achieve, it is a good idea to sit down and list the plants you want to grow and then lay them out in a plan, following the guidelines in this chapter to help you decide how to arrange them. Alternatively, start with a theme, such as a white border, and then plan the plants that could go into it. Such a plan need not be a precise drawing, nor a work of art. It is just a practical guide. It helps if you can draw your plan on graph paper to get some idea of scale, as then you will not be tempted to put too much into each bed.

Border Proportions

In a traditional cottage garden, plants were often simply planted where there were gaps. This gave a wonderful freedom, but smaller plants were often hidden by taller ones in front of them. Nowadays, borders tend to be a bit more disciplined, with taller plants at the back and shorter ones at the front. But there is more to laying out a border than this.

Below

A textbook example of how to plant a border with tall plants at the back and low ones at the front.

Depth

The depth of a border is important as the deeper it is, the taller the plants you can grow in it. Growing tall plants in a narrow border tends to look wrong. It rarely works, although as with all principles of gardening, there are always plenty of exceptions, and one of these is if the border is backed by a high wall or hedge. Generally speaking, though, the width or depth of a border should be at least twice the height of its tallest plants.

Generously deep beds always seem more pleasing to look at than narrow ones. Whatever the size of the garden, it will look more effective with fewer deeper beds than a greater number of narrow beds; think big. And, of course, deep beds allow a wider variety of plants to be included, and in greater numbers, which makes arranging the plants much easier. It also allows herbaceous plants to be set out in drifts, creating a better overall effect than with single planting.

Above
Plants with strong shapes,
like this eye-catching young
yucca, make ideal
specimens among softer
foliage.

Height

The general principle with beds that have a
background is to plant the tallest plants at the
back and shortest at the front. In island beds,
the tallest go in the middle with the shorter
plants surrounding them. However, if you follow
this rule blindly the border ends up looking like
choir stalls with even ranks of plants graded by
height. This not only becomes boring, but also
tends to make the eye move straight toward the
end of the bed without appreciating the plants
in between. Bring a few of the taller plants
forward, so that the overall impression becomes
a little more uneven. There are some tall plants,
such as *Verbena bonariensis* and many of the
grasses, which although they are tall, are thin
and wiry and allow you to see through them
with the plants beyond appearing in a haze.
Plant a few of these at the front to break up the
rigid lines of the border even more. One
advantage of pulling forward some of the taller
plants is that they will obscure what lies beyond,
which is not revealed until you have moved a bit
farther down the border, making the design
more exciting.

Border Proportions

A formal arrangement broken by bringing forward a few taller plants.

Plants arranged in a formal graduation, like a choir,
toward the back of the border.

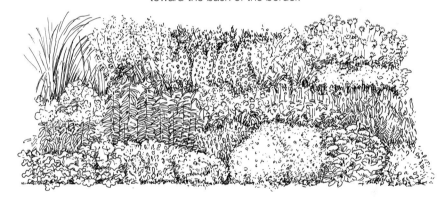

A few tall plants blocking the view, creating an air of mystery.

Positioning Plants

Good design in a border is as much about how you arrange the plants as it is about the plants you choose. If you have the luxury of a deep border, this task will be made much easier as you will be able to use groups of the same plant, rather than using plants singly. Using single plants can leave a bed looking spotty and rather cluttered.

When planting a group, always try to use an odd number of plants as these are much more easy to arrange than an even number. Once you get above nine it is not so important, but three or five plants are always much easier to lay out than four or six. The best effect is achieved by creating seemingly random drifts of plants which interlock to fill the space. As already mentioned, vary the heights a little to make the display more interesting. The most important point is to be bold: use large drifts for the best effect.

Right
A grass path between an avenue of variable-height blue- and yellow-flowered plants.

Positioning Plants

As a general principle, place taller plants at the back of the border. At the same time, plants make better groupings if they are planted in odd numbers. A group of two or four often seems awkward whereas three or five have a more pleasing look about them.

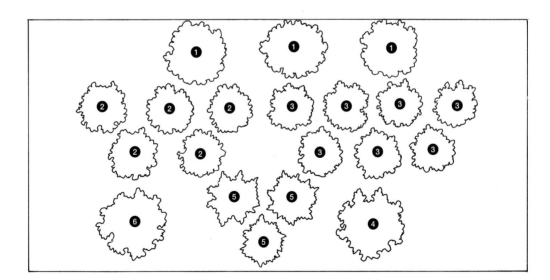

Key to Planting

1   *Verbascum bombyciferum*
2   *Anchillea* 'Gold Plate'
3   *Ligularia* 'The Rocket'
4   *Inula ensifolia*
5   *Hieracium lanatum*
6   *Lysimachia nummularia* 'Aurea'

Specimen Plants

Angelica archangelica **Angelica**
Architectural biennial herb with large
green, spherical flower heads in summer

***Cedrus deodara* 'Aurea'**
Small-to-medium, upright conifer with soft
feathery, golden-green foliage

Cordyline australis
A palm forming a rosette of strap-shaped
leaves

Crambe cordifolia
A perennial that produces enormous airy
heads of white flowers in summer

Cynara cardunculus **Cardoon**
A large perennial with huge crinkle-edged
silver leaves and large purple flowers in
summer

Fatsia japonica
An upright evergreen shrub with large
glossy, divided leaves

Gunnera manicata **Giant rhubarb**
A very large, moisture-loving perennial with
enormous leaves

***Hakonechloa macra* 'Aureola'**
Medium grass forming a fountain of
striped yellow and green foliage that turns
red in autumn

Matteuccia struthiopteris
Shuttlecock fern
Large fern that forms a neat fan of foliage

Miscanthus sinensis
'Zebrinus' Zebra grass
A large handsome grass forming upright
clumps of striped foliage.

Phormium tenax
A large perennial forming clumps of
sword-shaped leaves in eye-catching
colors

Yucca gloriosa
A large perennial forming a stiff rosette of
spiky leaves

Above

Plant shapes and colors are repeated to create rhythm in this lively border.

Specimen plants

Although most plants in a border should be planted in drifts, stunning effects can be created by using some plants singly as specimen plants to add focal points to the scheme. The plants best suited to this are those with a distinctive shape or texture that will stand out from the surrounding plants. Use these intermittently down the border to create rhythm (see below) or at the end of the border to add a definite full stop. These types of plants can also be used to highlight a feature such as an arbor or gateway, by being planted on either side. When planting the border, leave enough space around these varieties so that they really stand out. Choose spiky plants, such as cordylines and yuccas, or plants with a distinctive upright habit, such as grasses, columnar conifers, or even a clump of the gigantic gunnera.

Rhythm

In cottage-garden and other informal borders, everything can be a bit of a mixture, which is interesting in its own right. But one way to create a more formal sense of interest is by creating rhythm down the length of the border. This can be done by repeating particular plants or colors. Topiaried box bushes or bay trees will produce this effect, but there are many other more subtle ways of doing it. These include the repeated use of color and the use of related shapes of plants, such as those with spiky or cascading foliage, cordylines for example. Formal bedding schemes often take this technique to the extreme, by repeating patterns as well as colors and shapes.

Sometimes the effect is not so much a rhythm, more of a being led on. For example, one group of colors may lead naturally to the next. Dark blue flowers might merge into plants with pale blue ones, which in turn merge into white and on to creamy yellow and so on, creating natural progression.

Successional Interest

Most border plants are at their best in summer, but you will get more pleasure from your border if you can extend this period of interest into the other seasons, so that there is always something to enjoy. The downside of this is that the summer display will undoubtedly be less impressive, but with careful planning it should still be impressive enough. The secret to extending the season of interest is to use a wide variety of different plants. A border planted entirely with herbaceous perennials will be restricted to a few weeks in the summer, but introduce some early bulbs and a few shrubs for autumn color and winter structure, and you will have a feast for the eyes all year round.

Start the year with snowdrops, crocuses and early daffodils popping up among the flowering hellebores. Soon after, the emerging leaves of the herbaceous perennials can be enhanced with tulips, self-sown forget-me-nots, and the early perennial doronicums. Next comes the main bulk of the perennials, filling the border with color throughout the season, but don't forget to include a few later-flowering plants, such as asters and gloriosa daisies.

As the autumn approaches and the bright colors subside, the more structural and textural perennials become apparent. But the real highlights are the shrubs with their autumn tints and fruits, such as rose hips and berries. Winter is bound to be sparser, but again, the shrubs and small trees add structure, especially if they are evergreen. Color can be provided by the colored bark and stems of dogwoods, for example, and a few winter-flowering shrubs, like the daphnes and winter-flowering heathers. In the winter the main structure of the trees and shrubs remains. This is particularly noticeable with evergreens. The herbaceous borders have died down, but the remains of the dead stems and foliage still create color and form in the borders.

Below
The varying forms and textures of these seemingly lifeless plants provide winter interest.

Flower color

The one thing that most people consider more important than anything else in a border is flower color. Many are blind to the colors and textures of the foliage, but these must be taken into account as well, as the color of individual flowers rarely stands in isolation; it is the interaction with its neighbors that is important. Without this interaction a border really ceases to be a border with any great merit.

Overall image

There are at least two ways of looking at a border. The first is the overall impression and the second is the effect of individual plants or clumps of plants. The overall image is particularly important, as this is what you notice first and what you are likely to remember. In a way it is like an Impressionist painting, where you remember the feeling and mood but not the precise detail.

If colors are dotted around with little thought as to how they combine with their neighbors, the overall picture is spotty and very restless to the eye; it is not very harmonious. On the other hand, if colors that blend together are chosen and they are planted in drifts rather than one here and one there, they will merge into a restful overall picture.

Using color

As we will see later in more detail, color can be used in a number of different ways. First, it can set the tone and mood of a border. Soft pastel colors will give a romantic, hazy image, whereas a border full of hot vibrant colors is exhilarating and exciting. A peaceful image can also be created by selecting plants all of one color, making a scheme without conflict between different colors. White borders are a good example of this.

Soft and cool colors tend to look distant, and this effect can be used for making a border look longer than it is. Plant pale blues, for example, at the end of the border and it will have the same effect as hills looking farther away on a hazy day than they do on a bright one. On the other hand, if you plant bright reds in the distance they appear to be nearer than they really are. Bright colors also tend to draw the eye and so they can act as a focal points in the center of a border, for example, or to highlight a feature such as an obelisk.

Drifts of color

Colors work best in drifts or large patches. In perennial borders these tend to look best if each clump or drift is irregular in shape with no hard lines. Drifts do not have to be enormous. In a very small garden, three plants can constitute a drift and will look much better than a single plant. Merge the adjacent colors into a drift to create a soft patchwork. If two colors do not sit happily together but you still wish to use them, soften the boundary line by growing a clump of neutral foliage between them.

Choosing plants for color

Unfortunately, choosing plants for their colors is fraught with dangers. For example, if you like the look of a plant in a book, you may discover when it first flowers in your garden that it is nowhere near the same color as on the page. It is important to have seen the flower itself before deciding to buy the plant.

Another problem is that the name of a plant does not guarantee its color. Plants that have been propagated vegetatively, that is by cuttings or division, will be identical to the parent plant. If they have been grown from seed, however, then variation in size, habit, and flower color is possible and in many cases likely. If the choice of color is critical, always try to see the plant in flower before you buy it, just to check that it is what you want.

Right
Exciting color contrasts such as the contrast between these bright tulips and dark violas should be used wisely.

Foliage Color

Foliage is often overlooked when considering color in the garden, but it is very important. Indeed there are some gardens that are designed entirely around foliage rather than plants, partly on the basis that foliage generally lasts longer than flowers, and partly because in some ways you can get a greater subtlety with foliage.

Greens

Most foliage is green, but there are a large number of different greens. This is particularly apparent in spring when the leaves are all freshly unfurled. Most green foliage acts as a background or a permanent feature in the garden against which all other colors are displayed. Occasionally it plays a more dominant role, especially in single-colored borders. For example, in a white border there is green as well as white. The green here is more than just a mere background and must be chosen with care.

Purple and blue

Purple foliage is common in many gardens. There are not a great number of plants that have such leaves, but those that do are used extensively. Purple is a heavy color and must be used carefully. It relieves the monotony of green and can act as a perfect foil to a variety of flower colors, in particular purples, reds, and pinks. However, it should be used sparingly. A bank of purple-leaved shrubs, for example, can look very heavy and leaden; it is too somber and will be much improved by the addition of some green foliage.

Blue foliage is less common than purple. It is rarely true blue, but more of a steely color. There are several grasses in particular that have leaves of this color, as well as a few hostas. They mix well with blue or, as a contrast, yellow flowers.

Left
Purple-leaved shrubs need to be lightened by grouping them with green foliage or they may look heavy and dull.

Pale foliage

There are some plants that have gold or yellow foliage. On the whole these are not very vigorous plants, as the leaves are lacking in the chlorophyl, which not only makes the leaves green but also helps provide the energy on which plants grow. Plants that have these colors are often open to sun scorch and are best planted in areas of the garden where there is light shade. This is also good from an aesthetic point of view as these pale leaves will brighten up the shade. The paler colors, however, are more useful in their variegated form, where they are combined with green.

Variegated foliage

There is a large range of variegated foliage. The most common are green and yellow, green and cream, or green and white. Such plants can either have green leaves with the other color slashed on them, or green centers with a colored edge, or vice versa. In some cases the variegation is very subtle. For example, in some grasses the variegation is a very thin stripe down the margins of the leaves, while in others it is quite brash with the variegation predominating in the overall effect.

Variegated plants are very colorful and are especially useful in lightening a dark corner. However, too many in one place can be rather overpowering and restless to the eye. Use them with discretion.

Other variegations include greens with purples and reds. These are often mixed with cream as well as green so that you have a triple variegation. These plants tend to be interesting in their own right rather than creating a great splash of color, but there are a few that stand out from the crowd.

Above
Bergenia leaves are interesting at all times of the year, but especially so in winter.

Plant Shapes and Textures

Although color is the most prominent aspect of a border and the thing we notice first, the shape and texture of plants also play an important role in good border design and can be used to create interest.

Right

The upright spikes of *Kniphofia hooperi* provide a strongly colored vertical emphasis.

Plant shape

The outline of every plant is unique: some are tall and thin, while others are flat and ground-covering; some are squat and rounded, while others have cascading leaves like a fountain. These shapes should be used to create an interesting and diverse picture in the border.

Low plants

Prostrate plants tend to let the eye skate over them. A whole bed of such plants is boring and in need of something to break the monotony. However, they are perfect as linking passages between other more interesting plants. Low-growing plants can also be effective when allowed to flow over surface features so that their own surface becomes sculptural. Rounded and dome-shaped plants, on the other hand, have a self-contained, rather contented feel about them. They are comfortable plants to have in a border and contrast well with more spiky ones. They are useful for forming the basic structure of the border.

Below

A contrasting mixture of shapes and heights keeps the viewer's interest right along this border.

Plant Shapes

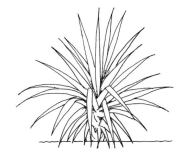

Fan-shape

Open fan-shaped

Weeping

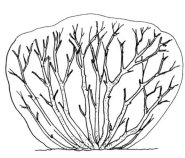

Upright bowl-shaped

Upright

Horizontally layered

Rounded

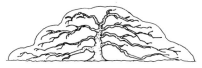

Mounded

Upright plants

Many plants have stiff stems that list slightly away from the center, roughly forming a fan as they spread out to find the light. These have a certain vertical emphasis and act as a good contrast to rounded shapes. Others have a very narrow base and leaves that curve upward and outward and downward, almost as if they were a fountain. These are dramatic plants and often catch the eye. Both types are best used in isolation rather than in groups so that their shape can be appreciated. Yet others have rigid leaves that tend to splay outward in a spiky spray or ball. They are very dramatic and should be used as focal points.

Any tall shape emphasizes the vertical in a border, but tall thin ones are especially useful for this. They are sometimes used as focal points and certainly play a part in the overall silhouette of the border.

Leaf shapes

As well as the shape of the whole plant, it is important that the shape of the leaves is also taken into consideration. Some directly influence the shape of the plant, such as strap-like leaves forming a fountain, or pointed ones forming a halo of spikes. But there are also filigree leaves, such as those of many ferns, which have a delicate nature, contrasting with the rounded, leathery leaves of hostas, for example. A mixture of leaf shapes is always more interesting than a border made up of one type.

Plant textures

The texture of plants is perhaps not so obvious as other aspects, but it does play a related and important part when designing a border. The texture mainly refers to individual parts of the plant such as the leaves, or in some cases the bark, but it can also relate to the plant as a whole, as the sum of the parts comes into play.

Foliage texture

One of the most obvious foliage textures is shiny. The leaves on these plants tend to reflect light and even sparkle. They are ideal plants for placing in darker corners where the light catching the leaves is reflected back, illuminating the gloom.

Foliage with deep ribs and prominent veins always looks interesting. These features break up the flat surface and allow light to be reflected from a variety of angles. This will often have the effect that a plain green leaf will appear to consist of several different greens. Some leaves are so folded that they appear pleated and are particularly attractive and eye-catching. This richness, as with most patterns, gives the viewer something to think about and appreciate, especially if it is intricate.

Above
The soft velvety texture of the *Cosmos atrosanguineus* is shown to great advantage against the feathery, silver foliage of the artemisia.

Many plants have their leaves covered in dense hairs, usually to protect them from the sun, rain, insects, or something else that threatens their existence. These hairs usually produce leaves that have a furry feel to them and provide them with such names as "lamb's ears" (*Stachys byzantina*). Such leaves have a double benefit of color and texture; the color is usually silver or gray. Both the texture and the color are perfect for linking colors and cooling them down. For example, they go well with bright magenta, a color not generally easy to cope with.

Other leaves have a matte or even velvety texture that absorbs light. This gives the leaves a richness and depth of color. Although frequently interesting in their own right, they work particularly well as linking passages between other more colorful plants.

Flower texture

The texture of the flowers has much the same effect as that of the foliage. Shiny petals are somehow exciting. They reflect the light, which lifts the color and makes it sparkle. On the other hand, velvet-textured petals have a sumptuous feeling about them, particularly if they are colored deep red. These create a rich and very luxurious effect which is somehow rather satisfying.

Another way in which flowers are textured is that they have lines or stripes, or dots and splashes on the flowers, which often draw you into the flower in the same way that they intend to guide the bee to the nectar. The texture of flowers is most noticeable when flowers occur in drifts, but it is most appreciated when the flowers are seen close up, when cut or at the border's edge.

Below
The irregularly cut petals of this tulip create quite a different flower from standard black tulips.

Types of Plant

A border can be made up of many different types of plants, and each will create a different effect. Most borders tend to contain a mixture these days, but shrub borders, herbaceous borders, and alpine beds are still popular.

Herbaceous perennials

Herbaceous plants are often the glory of the garden and form the body of most borders. The choice of plants is extremely wide, allowing great scope for planning and making a border. The big disadvantage of all-herbaceous borders is that they are essentially a summer feature, extending from early summer through into the autumn. For the rest of the year they are empty. However, their summer glory is so great that the winter's rest only heightens the anticipation for the following year.

Herbaceous plants are those that die back below ground each autumn and reappear in spring. They vary from the ground-hugging to giants that grow to a height of up to 10 feet (3 m) or more. Most are grown for their flowers, but some are also grown for their attractive foliage. On the whole, individual perennials do not have a particularly long flowering season. This may be seen as a disadvantage, but in fact it means the appearance of the border is always changing.

It should never become boring as the scene can change almost daily. It is possible to have a border in the early part of the year that is made up of, say, yellow and blue flowers, while the same border in autumn may be red and purple. There is plenty of scope for the gardener's imagination and skills.

After years of neglect, traditional herbaceous borders are once more making a comeback. They passed out of fashion when cheap and plentiful labor was no longer available in the garden. Herbaceous borders were thought of as time-consuming, but now it has been realized that if they are thoroughly worked over during the winter, the amount of time spent on them for the rest of the year is minimal, mainly restricted to deadheading and cutting back fading foliage. The time and effort put into creating herbaceous borders is well worth it; of all the border types they are the most satisfying to create.

Bulbs

Bulbs are invaluable in a border, popping up and adding splashes of color and interest throughout the year, often when little else is in flower. They take up very little space and will grow up through other plants, dying down again after flowering, to rest until the following year.

There are bulbs suitable for all styles of border. Smart lily-flowered tulips, for example, can be used in regimented groups in a formal border, while alliums can be dotted around between herbaceous plants in an abundant, relaxed scheme to add color and interest. Large bulbous plants, such as lilies and foxtail lilies, which produce towering spikes of color, can make great focal points, adding dazzling color and shape to the border. On the other hand, tiny cyclamen or crocuses can create dainty patches of intricate appeal in the depths of winter when little else is around.

Right
Bedding plants lend themselves to formal arrangements more than any other type of plant.

Key to Planting

1	*Macleaya cordata*	7	*Thalictrum flavum* 'Glauca'	13	*Campanula persicifolia*	21	*Geranium* 'Patricia'	27	*Persicaria affinis*
2	*Euphorbia charachias* subsp. *wulfenii*	8	*Aster novae-angliae* 'Andenken an Alma Pötschke'	14	*Echinops ritro*	22	*Heuchera micrantha* var. *diversifolia* 'Palace Purple'*	28	*Dianthus* 'Doris'
3	*Cephalaria gigantea*			15	*Verbena bonariensis*	23	*Pennisetum villosum*	29	*Stachys byzantina*
4	*Eupatorium purpureum* subsp. *maculatum* 'Atropurpureum'	9	*Sidalcea* 'Rose Queen'	16	*Penstemon* 'Andenken an Friedrich Hahn'	24	*Geranium riversleaianum* 'Mavis Simpson'	30	*Erysimum* 'Bowles Mauve'
		10	*Helenium* 'Moerheim Beauty'	17	*Aster x frikartii* 'Mönch'	25	*Bergenia cordifolia* 'Purpurea'	31	*Sedum telephium* subsp. *maximum* 'Atropurpureum'
5	*Crambe cordifolia*	11	*Monarda* 'Cambridge Scarlet'	18	*Geranium* 'Sue Crug'			32	*Geranium sanguineum*
6	*Achillea* 'Coronation Gold'	12	*Hemerocallis* 'Catherine Woodbery'	19	*Cynara cardunculus*	26	*Anthemis punctata* subsp. *cupaniana*	33	*Nepeta x faassenii*
				20	*Sedum* 'Herbstfreude'				

Bedding plants

Annual bedding plants used to be extremely popular among many gardeners, but now their main use seems to have moved from the borders to hanging baskets, window boxes, and containers. However, there is still a strong case for bedding plants in borders and they are gradually making a comeback.

Annuals, strictly speaking, are those plants that germinate, flower, seed and die all within one year. However, the definition is usually broadened to contain biennials (whose life-cycle is two years), short-lived perennials (which are best grown for one year only), and tender perennials (plants that will not stand a winter outside and are thus treated as annuals). One of the big advantages of these plants is that they have a very long flowering season, producing a steady stream of blooms from early summer right through to the autumn.

The palette of colors available in bedding plants is enormous so gardeners can choose to create any kind of scheme they wish. If the plants chosen are grown inside or in a greenhouse until they are planted outside, they are likely to be in flower already, so that a bare bed can be transformed from bare soil to full floral glory in a matter of hours.

Flats or individual pots of annuals can be easily purchased from garden centers and nurseries; they are ready to use for instant effect, but you are limited in choice. In many cases they are only available in mixed colors. If you grow your annuals from seed, the range of plants is much greater and you can buy seeds of most plants that will produce a single color, making it easier to achieve individual designs.

Key to Planting

1	*Lithodora diffusa*	**7**	*Pulsatilla vulgaris*	**13**	*Oxalis laciniata*	**19**	*Dianthus* 'Pike's Pink'
2	*Dianthus glacialis*	**8**	*Narcissus* 'Tête-à-Tête'	**14**	*Gentiana verna*	**20**	*Linum* 'Gemmell's Hybrid'
3	*Penstemom pinifolius*	**9**	*Cyclamen coum*	**15**	*Fritillaria meleagris*	**21**	*Geranium dalmaticum*
4	*Diascia* 'Lilac Belle'	**10**	*Primula marginata*	**16**	*Juniperus communis* 'Compressa'	**22**	*Saxifraga* 'Southside Seedling'
5	*Saxifraga* 'Baldensis'	**11**	*Erinus alpinus*	**17**	*Lewisia cotyledon*	**23**	*Campanula cochleariifolia*
6	*Cyclamen hederifolium* 'Album'	**12**	*Saxifraga* 'Faldonside'	**18**	*Phlox douglasii* 'Crackerjack'	**24**	*Oxalis* 'Ione Hecker'

25	*Iris histrioides*
26	*Daphne cneorum* var. *pygmaea*

Shrubs and trees

There was a time when any misdoings in a novel, be they violent or sexual, took place in the shrubbery. Nowadays the term shrubbery seems almost to have disappeared, but still shrubs and trees are the backbone of our gardens, and many people use them almost exclusively as, theoretically, they need very little care and attention.

There is a tremendous range of trees and shrubs available today, which gives the gardener plenty of scope when designing a border. Factors to take into account include flowers and flower color; foliage color, shape and texture; and the tree or shrub's shape and general appearance. Some will have many distinct phases: the emerging spring foliage, flowers, summer foliage, fruit, colored autumn foliage, and winter bark and silhouette. Trees and shrubs form a permanent structure.

This means you can guarantee that there will always be something of interest in the border, whereas herbaceous plants and annuals will die back in the winter. The structure may be further reinforced by using evergreen trees and shrubs, which undergo less change during the year's cycle.

Once planted, trees and shrubs do not need a great deal of maintenance. Very few trees need pruning, except to restrict their size. However, most shrubs do benefit from it. They can be left, but they will become overgrown and full of old and dying wood. They will also lose their tendency to flower. The idea is to promote new growth from the base. To this end the rule of thumb is to remove up to a third of the wood each year, pruning it immediately after flowering. There are plenty of books that specialize in shrubs and these should be consulted for precise pruning details.

Alpines in borders

Growing true alpines is a bit of a specialist undertaking and these little plants tend to get lost in a normal border, especially when combined with other types of plants. However, there are many different levels at which to enjoy alpines, and although many people grow them for the plants themselves, others grow them simply for the effect. These gardeners choose the simpler plants that are easy to grow, yet still look stunning.

Two types of borders are suited to alpines and rock plants. The first is a traditional rock garden, which is designed to look like an outcrop of rock, and the other is a more formal raised bed. Rock gardens are simply borders that have been designed to act both visually and physically as the plants' native home. The rock and stone provide sharp drainage while giving protection to the plants. They also set them off visually, acting as a perfect backdrop to the small and often delicate plants. Raised beds are merely borders that are raised above ground level, making the plants easier to appreciate.

Growing alpines can become addictive, and before you know it, you may be growing more and more specialized plants that need a great deal of skill and expertise. These plants need to be grown in special conditions and half the skill in growing them is to recognize what these conditions are. A rock garden can be created that has all kinds of special nooks and crannies. Some plants need to be grown in vertical crevices while others like a more humus-rich soil and the slight shade found at the base of a rock. Creating such a complex border can be very absorbing.

Mixed borders

The one type of border that has become very popular is the mixed border. This allows the gardener to have the best of all the different types of plants, mixing together the various elements into one scheme. It allows the use of shrubs and trees to form a permanent structure, at the same time interplanting and underplanting with fresh-looking, colorful perennials and bulbs. Quick-growing and long-lasting annuals fill in the gaps and add constant color throughout the summer.

Except in larger borders, trees are not used a great deal. Some, however, such as ash, are perfect for creating height without being too overpowering. There are many shrubs that are suitable, varying from ground huggers such as heather (*Erica*) up to large shrubs such as philadelphus, which grow almost as tall as trees. On the whole smaller and medium-sized shrubs are the most useful, especially those that have attractive flowers and good foliage.

Perennials should always play a major part in a mixed border, adding the main color and texture. Since most perennials have a relatively short season, they give the border a changing image throughout the summer. This prevents the border from becoming boring, as there is always something new to see. Winter- and early-flowering plants, such as hellebores and

primroses, can be planted at the back of the border or among the deciduous shrubs so that they utilize areas that will be out of sight later in the season.

Annuals can be used in a mixed border to give color over a long period. They are particularly useful for filling in odd spaces. They are also ideal as a temporary filling for newly planted areas where the plants have not yet filled out and reached their ultimate size. There are many annuals that act more like perennials than the more common bedding plants. They have a fairly short flowering season and, although they die after flowering, they self sow so that they reappear the following year. These are very useful in a mixed border, although some may need weeding out if they start to spread beyond the area in which you want them to grow.

The elements of the mixed border should blend together well. When arranging the plants, try not only to get adjacent colors that go well together, but also to spread the different flowering times evenly across the border, so that it looks as full in autumn as it does in spring and summer. Keep a few annuals in pots in reserve and quickly plant them should a barren area appear.

Below
Mixed borders change character with the seasons, providing unique displays throughout the year.

Color Themes

The use of color in the garden is not much different from its use in the house: the essence is to bring together a combination that is pleasing, something that we feel comfortable in. So it is with borders. In the garden, the principle is to harmonize the colors so that a restful or arresting image is created, drifting from one set of colors easily into the next, perhaps accenting here or there with a brighter or contrasting color. However, not all schemes need be mixed; many successful borders have been created using a single color.

Single-colored borders may seem a simple idea but creating them is not as easy as it sounds. The number of variations on each color is enormous, and they do not all necessarily combine well. Colors often have two different sides; for example, yellows can either have a touch of green or a touch of red in their makeup. The two do not combine satisfactorily in the same border. The same can be said of the purple-reds and the orange-reds.

In practice there is no such thing as a single-colored border. The flowers may all be one color, but there is always the foliage as well. This is no bad thing, as a border of unrelenting yellow or red, for example, would be too much to take in. The foliage creates a background against which the color stands out and also acts as a buffer between two areas of a slightly different color that would not work together.

Two-colored borders are an extension of the single-color idea. Here two sympathetic colors can be chosen to harmonize, or contrasting colors can be used to create a bit of excitement. Popular schemes include white and yellow and yellow and blue. In some schemes one color can be predominant while the other is just a dash to catch the eye, or the colors can be mixed in roughly equal proportions.

As well as one- or two-colored borders, it is possible to have multicolored borders that are still selective. Soft pastel colors, for example, are very popular and can be combined to make a restful picture. As a complete contrast, a border of hot vibrant colors such as reds, oranges, and golds will set the pulse racing.

White Borders

The white border has become very popular, and it is one of the most satisfying borders to create.

Key to Planting

1	Pyrus salicifolia 'Pendula'	8	Aquilegia vulgaris 'Nivea'	14	Cyclamen hederifolium	21	Dianthus 'Haytor White'
2	Anemone nemorosa	9	Galanthus nivalis	15	Epilobium angustifolium var. album	22	Viola cornuta 'Alba'
3	Lunaria annua 'Alba Variegata'	10	Anemone x hybrida 'Honorine Jobert'	16	Lilium longiflorum	23	Salvia officinalis 'Alba'
4	Campanula latifolia var. alba			17	Onopordum acanthium	24	Nicotiana sylvestris
5	Lysimachia clethroides	11	Geranium phaeum 'Album'	18	Lychnis coronaria 'Alba'	25	Tulipa 'White Triumphator'
6	Digitalis purpurea f. albiflora	12	Argyranthemum frutescens	19	Stachys byzantina	26	Antirrhinum (white variety)
7	Cosmos bipinnatus 'Purity'	13	Convolvulus cneorum	20	Ornithogalum umbellatum	27	Petunia (white variety)

28	Silene uniflorum
29	Lamium maculatum 'White Nancy'
30	Cerastium tomentosum

The nature of white

White is a very complex color; in fact, strictly speaking, it is not a color but rather the absence of color. Theoretically there is only one white, pure white, but in reality white varies considerably, as a look around the room will show. The paper on this page is white, as is the ceiling of your room probably, or perhaps the painted woodwork around the window. Compare them beside one another and the point will be made. The same white will also look completely different in different contexts. For example, look at the paper of this page against a brown desk or dark carpet and it will look very white; compare it with fresh gloss paint and it will appear darker and much more subdued.

The character of white

White holds a special place in the world of color. It has always had a special meaning, representing peace, tranquillity, purity, chastity, and cleanliness. White birds and animals have always held a special place in folklore, while white flowers are still used in special ceremonies where peace and purity are present, such as funeral and wedding rituals. A white border has all these qualities: it is a tranquil, peaceful place, a place for sitting and contemplation. It has none of the hurly-burly of modern life. It also has the ability to shine out in the dusk, making it an ideal setting for those who mainly use their gardens in the evening. Coincidentally, many white flowers are heavily fragrant in the evening, another reason for using them in areas where you sit or relax.

Shades of white

The art of creating a white border is to mix the various shades to allow for the glistening whites, the dull whites, and the creams. The best way to discover how the colors work is to see them in practice. Visit gardens with white borders, such as the world-famous one at Sissinghurst Castle in Kent, England.

Enhancing white

It is impossible to have a purely white border, short of stripping off all the foliage from the plants. Many such borders are a mixture of green and white and most also include plants with silver or gray foliage. The greens not only act as a background, but their yellow content links well with the yellow of creams. The silvers, similarly, are extremely effective as foils, their muted quality enhancing the brightness of the whites. Often silver plants may have yellow or other colored flowers, but these can be removed before they open so that they do not spoil the effect.

Contrasts

For sudden impact, add a splash of a bright color such as red or blue amid all the white. This will immediately draw the eye and will emphasize the whiteness of the rest of the border. But do this with care; do not overdo it or it will spoil the effect rather than enhance it. A red among white is a stark contrast, a pink is a more subtle one. It is often a question of trial and error: try placing pots of plants in flower in the border before planting them.

Below

White borders are not strictly borders of a single color, they also involve the greens and grays of the foliage, but the white is dominant.

White flowers

Japanese anemone
A medium-height perennial with dish-shaped flowers in pure white in late summer

Anthemis punctata subsp. *cupaniana*
A low-growing perennial with flowers in spring to summer

Choisya ternata **Mexican orange**

blossom
A medium shrub with fragrant flowers in summer

Clematis **'Marie Boisselot'**
A tall climber with showy summer flowers

Dianthus **'Haytor White' Pink**
A low-growing perennial covered with flowers in summer

Leucanthemum x *superbum* **'Everest'**
A medium-height perennial with daisy-like flowers in summer

Nicotiana sylvestris
A statuesque annual with late summer or autumn flowers

Philadelphus **'Manteau d'Hermine'**
Mock orange
A small-to-medium, scented, summer-flowering shrub

Pulmonaria officinalis **'Sissinghurst White'**
A low-growing perennial with valuable flowers in winter to spring

Rosa **'Iceberg'**
A medium-height rose with pure white flowers in summer

Tulipa **'White Triumphator'**
A particularly spectacular tulip with bright white spring flowers

Viola cornuta **'Alba Minor'**
A carpeting perennial with dainty white flowers in spring and summer

Purple Borders

Purple is a rich color, often overlaid with the concept of luxury and royalty. Its richness comes from its mixture of red and blue. However, it is not as eye-catching nor as hot as red nor as cool as blue. It is a good solid color, with which most people feel comfortable and which combines well with many other colors.

Above

Borders composed solely of purple flowers and foliage can become a bit leaden; lighten them with a few other colors, especially gray foliage.

Purple flowers

There is quite a wide range of purple flowers, varying from the almost violet to the almost red. There are probably more on the bluer end than the red end, which is fortunate as these are the lively colors. The reds are deeper and more sumptuous but too much of them and they get boring, whereas most people seem to be more tolerant of the blue-purples. The red-purples, such as the burgundies, can feel rather heavy, a bit leaden or somber. They are fine in small quantities but in larger amounts they can kill the effect of the border. They can be lifted by planting them with silver foliage, and they mix well with bright reds as long as these do not have too much orange in them.

The blue-purples will go with a much wider range of colors. They are rarely vibrant, again being quite subdued. Although they are dark in color, they mix well with pastel colors as long as only a few are used; too many and the light airy look of the pastels will be subdued.

Purple foliage

There are a handful of plants with purple foliage. These make wonderful backgrounds against which to see both bright and softer colors. However, too much purple foliage on its own can become very dull. This particularly true of shrub foliage. If the border is mainly foliage, use purple to add interest and contrast, but use it sparingly. With the sun shining directly onto the leaves, purple foliage appears particularly dead. Yet if the sun is coming from behind, it can look truly spectacular. Each leaf glows and really comes alive, so try to site them to catch the late afternoon or evening sun.

Purple borders

A purple border is unusual, but great fun to create. There are one or two in famous gardens and these are well worth visiting, especially if you can locate one in your area where you can see it at different times of the year. The skill in making one comes in the mixing of the colors, using a few violets and some deep reds to broaden the spectrum. Use plants with purple foliage to help continue the theme through periods when there are not enough plants in flower to fill the whole border. They will also act as a good foil to many of the flowers. Plants with gray or silver foliage will often help lighten a purple border.

Below

Irises offer a wide range of colors, many of them very subtle. The flowers are large enough for their color to be fully appreciated.

Purple flowers

Aster amellus 'King George'
Aster
A medium perennial with daisy-like flowers in late summer to autumn

Clematis 'Mrs. N. Thompson'
A tall summer-flowering climber

Echinacea purpurea
A striking perennial, of medium height, with large daisy-like flowers in summer

Erysimum 'Bowles Mauve'
A perennial wallflower with a medium-height, bushy habit that flowers profusely in summer

Geranium pratense
A medium-height, perennial geranium with spring-to-summer flowers

Liatris spicata
A medium perennial with bottle-brush flower spikes in summer

Lythrum salicaria
A handsome medium perennial with purple flowers in summer

Osteospermum jucundum
A low-growing tender perennial, usually grown as an annual, which flowers in summer

Penstemon 'Russian River'
A prolific-flowering, upright perennial with flower spikes appearing in summer and autumn

Primula denticulata
A short clump-forming perennial related to the primrose, with purple drumstick flower heads in spring

Salvia splendens Cleopatra Series
Short spiked annuals with purple flowers throughout summer

Verbena bonariensis
A tall, airy perennial, which will seed around the border, producing flowers in late summer and autumn

Purple foliage

Acer palmatum f. atropurpureum
Japanese maple
A small tree or large shrub with handsome, divided foliage

Ajuga reptans 'Atropurpurea'
A ground-hugging perennial with shiny foliage

Berberis thunbergii f. atropurpurea
A striking shrub with tiny leaves and a spreading habit

Cordyline australis 'Atropurpurea'
A purple-leaved palm that will eventually grow into a small tree, perfect as a focal point

Cotinus coggygria 'Royal Purple'
Smoke bush
A medium shrub with rounded leaves that turn a rich red in autumn

Dahlia 'Bishop of Llandaff'
A large bulb with purple-black foliage and bright red flowers in late summer

Foeniculum vulgare 'Purpureum'
Bronze fennel
A tall, upright perennial with very feathery purple foliage

Phormium tenax Purpureum Group
A medium-to-tall perennial with leathery, evergreen sword-shaped leaves in red-purple

Ricinus communis 'Gibsonii'
An impressive annual with huge glossy leaves

Salvia officinalis Purpurascens Group
Purple sage
A low-growing evergreen shrub

Sedum 'Vera Jameson'
A low-growing perennial with fleshy purple foliage and late-summer flowers

Vitis vinifera 'Purpurea'
The ornamental purple grape vine, a tall climber with very decorative foliage

Yellow and Blue Borders

Yellow is a cheerful, sparkling color. It has the feeling of spring about it and tends to lift the spirits. Blue, on the other hand, is a more solid color, especially bright blue, but it has the ability to be luminous especially, curiously enough, at the end of the day as the light fades. Both colors have variants that make them warm or cool depending on how much red they have mixed into them. They are contrasting colors and as such make a very fresh-looking border when used together.

Yellow

There are two types of yellow: those that tend toward orange and those that are more inclined toward green. The orange-yellows and the golds are warm colors, whereas the greener ones are much cooler. If the warmer colors have white in them, then peach and buttery tones are present. These are valuable pastel colors in the garden. The hot yellows tend to dominate other colors and should be used sparingly if they are not to overwhelm the other flowers in the border. This is the color to which the eye is first drawn. Place it in the middle of an area with nothing else in flower and the whole space will be illuminated to such an extent that the lack of other flowers is unlikely to be noted. Attempt this with, say, blue, and the surroundings become much more apparent.

The softer yellows, with their slightly green tinge, are much cooler—in some cases almost icy in their feel. These are the ones that associate best with the cool blues. They also work remarkably well with silver foliage, an unlikely combination, but one that is well worth trying.

Yellow is one of the most common colors among flowers and there is a tremendous range to choose from, varying from ground-hugging plants such as *Lysimachia nummularia* to the gigantic vertical spires of some of the mulleins (*Verbascum*).

Right
A symphony of yellows and blues with a subtle use of variegated foliage to create the background.

Blue

Pure blue is a cool color. This makes it much easier to use than the more dominant reds and yellows. It combines well without standing out too much and thus perhaps distorting the overall effect in its favor, as do the other dominant colors. The one time that it does come into its own is during twilight. As the day fades into darkness, the blues take on a luminescence that leaves them still surprisingly visible well after other colors have disappeared.

As with yellow, there are two sides to blue. When mixed with a touch of red, it becomes violet and this is a warmer color. On the other hand, as the blue becomes lighter, it cools even further. The pale blues are ideal companions for other pastel colors. Bright, true blue will also combine well with pastels as it is not dominant enough to swamp them, but is strong enough to create areas of interest. It combines well with the cooler yellows.

Yellow and blue borders

While both yellow and blue will combine well with most other colors, they look especially good when a border of just the two colors is created. Although the warmer colors can be used, the cooler yellows and blues really go together well. The yellow intensifies the blue and so they become equal partners in what usually turns out to be a very fresh border. The flowers have a clear-cut quality about them and it is very refreshing to look at in contrast to mixed borders.

Do not go overboard and plant all the borders in such a scheme; as refreshing as it is in small doses, it can become boring in quantity. One border—or more if it is a small enclosed area or a garden within a garden—is usually sufficient.

Yellow flowers

Achillea 'Coronation Gold'
A medium-tall perennial with flat golden flower heads in summer

Aurinia saxatilis
A low-growing, spring-flowering annual

Cephalaria gigantea
A tall, summer-flowering perennial

Cestrum parqui
A medium-tall shrub with flowers in summer to autumn

Fremontodendron californicum
A large, sprawling climber with cup-shaped golden flowers in summer

Helianthus annuus Sunflower
A tall, late-flowering annual

Hemerocallis 'Corky' Daylily
A lovely summer-flowering perennial with yellow flowers

Lysimachia nummularia 'Aurea'
A carpeting perennial with yellow foliage and summer flowers

Narcissus 'Peeping Tom'
A small, spring-flowering daffodil

Primula vulgaris Primrose
A small, spring-flowering perennial

Rosa 'Graham Thomas'
A medium-height yellow rose with flowers in summer and autumn

Verbascum bombyciferum
A tall, upright, architectural biennial with yellow flowers above silver foliage

Blue flowers

Agapanthus
A medium-height perennial with spiky foliage and rich blue flowers in summer

Ajuga reptans
A carpeting perennial with glossy leaves and blue flowers in spring to summer

Aster amellus
A late-flowering, medium-height perennial with daisy-like flowers

Campanula persicifolia
A medium-height perennial with bell-shaped blue flowers in summer

Delphinium grandiflorum 'Blue Butterfly'
A tall-growing perennial with spikes of blue flowers in summer

Eryngium alpinum
A small-to-medium perennial with little blue daisy flowers in summer

Felicia amelloides
A great container plant with vivid blue, daisy-like flowers

Iris reticulata
A tiny bulb with blue iris flowers in winter and early spring

Meconopsis betonicifolia Himalayan poppy
A medium-height perennial with true blue flowers in summer

Nepeta racemosa
A low-medium perennial covered in clear blue flowers in summer and autumn

Salvia officinalis Sage
A medium shrub with blue flowers in summer and handsome grayish foliage that sets them off well

Veronica spicata
A low-growing, dainty perennial with bright blue flowers in summer

Soft Romantic Schemes

It is difficult to define exactly what people mean when they refer to a romantic garden. It may just be the neatness—everything in its place, neat and tidy. On the other hand, it may be the design of the garden with bowers wreathed in swags of roses or honeysuckle. However variable the vision, one aspect tends to remain constant: the colors. A romantic garden consists of soft, ethereal colors, highlighted with occasional splashes of a deeper color, usually red.

Key to Planting

1   *Rosa rugosa*
2   *Solanum jasminoides* (growing over arch)
3   *Delphinium* 'Crown Jewel'
4   *Stachys byzantina*
5   *Anemone* x *hybrida*
6   *Galega officinalis*
7   *Erysimum* 'Bowles Mauve'
8   *Verbena bonariensis*
9   *Sidalcea candida*
10 *Galactites tomentosa*
11 *Geranium riversleaianum* 'Mavis Simpson'
12 *Lavandula angustifolia*
13 *Dianthus* 'Doris'
14 *Diascia vigilis* 'Jack Elliott'
15 *Nepeta* x *faassenii*

Cool colors

Cool colors are the blues, the greens, the grays, and the whites. These are gentle on the eye, especially the paler versions of the colors. They tend to have a soothing, tranquil quality about them that makes them good for relaxing and hence for romance. They also tend to be receding colors: they appear farther away than they really are.

Pastel colors

Pastel colors are primary colors to which white has been added: the pinks, peaches, primroses, and lilacs. They are the soft colors that do not offend or assault the eye. They are easy to look

at because the white content gives them a linking theme so that they can act together without conflict.

Old-fashioned plants

Many of the more old-fashioned plants have a greater romantic feel about them than their modern equivalents. This is not necessarily because "old is better," but more to do with the shape and texture of the flower. Old-fashioned roses, for example, tend to look soft and more textured. Modern ones have far more clear-cut profiles and colors which may appear bold or contemporary. Even what would normally be a soft color appears quite harsh in modern

cultivars. Pink, for example, is often very bright, with overtones of magenta. They lose a lot of the subtlety of old-fashioned flowers.

Romantic borders

Romantic borders are those that look relaxed and thus make the viewer seem relaxed. They tend to be created for overall effect rather than for the interest that individual plants may create. The plants are chosen for the color and general effect they portray.

As with all planting, the border looks best if the plants are arranged in clumps or drifts, with the colors effortlessly blending with their neighbors.

However, unlike brighter colors, romantic colors can be dotted around to give the impression more of a haze. This is particularly true of wildflower meadows, where the misty quality is further enhanced by the grasses. Even in a more conventional border, grasses such as *Hordeum jubatum* can be used to create the same effect. The receding nature of cool colors and the softness of pastels means that a long border, even one planted in blocks of color, blurs into a haze of color the farther it gets from the viewer. The softer colors can be enhanced by having an occasional flash of a bright one such as red. A few red poppies, for example, in a wildflower border help to create just the right impression.

It is important to add height to romantic borders; they should be three-dimensional. Climbing roses can be very effective, especially if they are arranged as swags growing along ropes at the back or front of the border. A seat in the middle of the border surrounded by an arbor of roses or another fragrant climber will help to create the right atmosphere.

Fragrance is also an important adjunct to romantic color. The two go together perfectly for creating atmosphere. Again the old-fashioned plants, as opposed to modern hybrids, are the most likely to have fragrance.

Below
Magnolias may take a few years before they flower, but the lovely effect of the pink or white flowers is worth waiting for.

Mauve and lilac flowers

Aquilegia alpina
A low-growing perennial with endearing "granny's bonnet" flowers in spring

Aster sedifolius
A medium perennial with daisy-like flowers in late summer and autumn

Delphinium 'Crown Jewel'
A tall, summer-flowering perennial with stately spikes of lilac flowers

Galactites tomentosa
A low to medium-height, summer-flowering annual

Galega officinalis Goat's rue
Aa tall, summer-flowering perennial

Hosta fortunei
Although these perennials are best known for their foliage, they have elegant summer flowers.

Lavandula angustifolia Lavender
A medium-height shrub with purple flowers throughout summer

Nepeta faassenii Catmint
A low-growing perennial massed with lilac flowers in summer and autumn

Perovskia atriplicifolia
A medium-height subshrub with lilac flowers on gray stems in late summer and autumn

Polemonium reptans
A low-growing perennial with spikes of lilac flowers in spring or summer

Primula marginata
A low-growing perennial, related to the primrose, with mauve flowers above handsome grayish foliage in spring

Scabiosa caucasica
A medium-height, summer-flowering perennial with large open flowers

Pink flowers

Anemone x hybrida Japanese anemone
A medium-height perennial with cup-shaped flowers in late summer and autumn

Deutzia x elegantissima 'Rosealind'
A handsome shrub with pink flowers in summer

Dianthus 'Doris' Pink
A perennial forming clumps of spiky foliage and pink flowers in summer and autumn

Diascia vigilis
A low-growing perennial covered with pink flowers in summer

Geranium endressii
A medium-height, summer-flowering hardy geranium

Lamium maculatum 'Roseum'

Deadnettle
A low-growing perennial with variegated foliage and flowers in spring and summer

Monarda 'Croftway Pink' Bergamot
A medium-height perennial with shaggy flowers in summer

Papaver orientale 'Cedric Morris'
Oriental poppy
A perennial with huge pink flowers in early summer

Persicaria affinis
A low-growing, vigorous perennial with pink flowers in summer and autumn

Phuopsis stylosa
A very pretty, low-growing perennial with summer flowers

Sedum 'Herbstfreude'
A fleshy, medium-height perennial with clear pink flowers in autumn

Sidalcea
A medium-height perennial with spikes of pink flowers in summer

Bold, Exotic Schemes

At the other extreme from the soft, romantic colors are the bold, brash, hot colors. These scream for attention and immediately draw the eye. They do not form a romantic background, but are full of excitement. Like all excitement, however, these colors can become tiring after a while, so they should be used with a certain amount of caution.

Right
Bright color schemes must be handled sensitively or they can become garish and lose their attraction.

Hot colors

The hot colors are those that lie opposite the cool colors on the artist's color wheel. They are the flame reds, orange, gold, and yellow. They are all eye-catchers. They create bold statements and stand out in a crowd. Such colors can be used with individual plants as focal points to draw the eye, in groups to enhance an otherwise dull border, or mixed with other hot colors to create a whole border.

Warm colors

The hot colors are the extremes of a wider group known as the warm colors. These colors are welcoming and tend to create a warm feeling. They include soft colors such as pink, as well as the earthy colors of dried stems, seed heads and foliage. However, these softer colors

are not as powerful as the hotter ones and are of little use in hot exotic borders.

Reds

Reds with a touch of yellow are most reminiscent of flames and fire, and are thus the most exciting. They cover that part of the spectrum between pure red and orange. The reds on the other side, with blue in them, are warm, but they are not hot and exciting in the same way. The two sides of red do not mix satisfactorily and are best kept apart in the garden.

Yellows

The hot yellows are those between pure yellow and orange. These include the golds. The other

side of pure yellow is tinged with green and forms the cool yellows, which have no place in a hot border as they are likely to have the reverse effect, namely, to cool it down.

Orange

Orange is a mixture of yellow and red and is a good color for the hot border as it retains the eye-catching quality of both parents. In some of its paler manifestations, such as peach, it remains warm but loses its heat and excitement.

Hot foliage

There is very little red or orange foliage, outside of tropical houseplants and greenhouse plants. There is no reason why these should not be used in a hot border as long as they are planted outside only for the summer. There are many variegated plants, which include warm yellow or gold, that can be used. Green foliage has the advantage of hot colors standing out against it. It acts as a good foil, but too much will emphasize individual plants or clumps of plants and may swamp the bold overall feeling of the border.

Hot borders

Hot borders are fun. They are lively and exciting. The eye has plenty to look at and is constantly darting from one color to another. But like an exciting party, there comes a point when the eye has had enough and it wants to find some place quieter. It is therefore not a good idea to fill the whole garden with hot borders. Vary it with cooler ones and large areas of lawn, which will likewise give the eye somewhere peaceful to rest.

Hot colors are very good for making exotic borders created to imitate the tropics. The use of strong bold foliage and bright colors, using house plants for extra boost if necessary, can create a powerful illusion, especially in a small garden.

Below
The tissue-thin flowers of *Papaver nudicaule* combine delicate form with strong color.

Red flowers

Crocosmia 'Lucifer'
A tall-growing bulb forming large clumps of sword-shaped leaves and red flowers in late summer

Dahlia 'Bishop of Llandaff'
A medium-height bulb with red flowers in late summer and autumn

Eccremocarpus scaber
A medium-height climber with tubular red flowers in summer

Hemerocallis 'Stafford' Daylily
A medium-height perennial with large trumpet-shaped flowers in summer

Kniphofia rooperi
A medium-height perennial with spiky foliage and red-hot poker flowers in summer and autumn

Lychnis chalcedonica
A medium-height perennial with clear scarlet summer flowers

Mimulus cupreus 'Whitecroft Scarlet'
A low-growing perennial with prolific red flowers in summer

Monarda 'Cambridge Scarlet' Bergamot
A medium-height perennial with shaggy flowers in summer

Paeonia officinalis Peony
A medium-height perennial with huge, cup-shaped flowers in late spring to early summer

Potentilla 'Gibson's Scarlet'
A medium-height perennial that will scramble among other plants and produce scarlet flowers in summer

Rosa 'Parkdirektor Riggers'
A tall climbing rose with clear red flowers in summer and autumn

Tropaeolum speciosum
A tall climbing bulb with exotic-looking flowers in summer and autumn

Orange flowers

Alstroemeria aurea
A vigorous medium-height perennial with summer flowers

Anthemis sancti-johannis
A medium-height, summer-flowering perennial with daisy-like flowers

Canna 'Orange Perfection'
An exotic-looking perennial with large leathery leaves and orange flowers in summer

Crocosmia crocosmiiflora 'Emily McKenzie'
A medium-height bulb forming large clumps of spiky foliage and flowers in late summer to autumn

Geum 'Borisii'
A medium-height perennial that will scramble among other plants, with clear orange flowers in summer

Papaver orientale 'Harvest Moon' Oriental poppy
A perennial with huge flowers in early summer

Potentilla 'William Rollison'
A medium-height perennial with orange flowers in summer

Primula Polyanthus
A low-growing perennial with orange flowers in spring

Rhododendron 'Orange Beauty'
A medium-height shrub with orange spring flowers

Rudbeckia hirta
A medium-height perennial with large daisy-like flowers in late summer to autumn

Trollius
A low-to-medium growing perennial with orange flowers in spring

Tropaeolum majus Nasturtium
An annual climber or scrambler with large flowers in summer to autumn

Seasonal Borders

It may seem a cliché, but it is true nonetheless that when working in the garden, you are closer to nature. Above all you are much more aware of the seasons. To most people the summer is the summer, but to the gardener it has subseasons, each noted as certain plants come and go. However, watching the seasons is not just of passing interest, it is an important part of creating and understanding a garden.

Whatever border you design is going to look different with every season. The only possible exception is one filled with conifers, but even many of these subtly change color each season. It is possible to create individual gardens for certain times of year—for example, winter gardens, which show off a selection of plants that look good in winter. Such borders, however, rely on there being plenty of space. In the small garden it is a waste to devote a whole border just to the winter months, for example. The trick is to blend all the seasons together in one border so something is always happening.

Each season has its own individual feel. In spring the sap rises; the border is full of the atmosphere of regeneration. The flowers are bright and the foliage fresh. As the summer progresses, the border settles down with a solidity that is in keeping with coping with the hot sun. As the year wanes, the colors of the flowers and foliage begin to take on their autumn tints, with russets and golds playing a dominant part. Finally, the winter arrives, and a few hardy plants stick their noses above the soil with a sense of defiance. In the small garden, a border should be able to capture all these moods if it is to be of interest all year round.

Depending on the type of border, there are usually some elements that remain the same throughout the year. Trees and shrubs, for example, are permanent features, although they may change in detail as leaves and flowers come and go. However, evergreens form a really permanent feature around which everything else weaves. When planning a border, these fixed elements must be carefully considered. They will not only create a rigid visual structure to the border but will also afford frost protection in winter or shade in summer.

Spring

Spring is the time of rejuvenation and reemergence. One minute winter seems to be all around, then suddenly colorful plants thrust up through the soil and the spring has arrived. Often the gardener is caught unaware, and although nothing is more welcome than spring flowers, particularly after a long winter, it is also the time of year when it is important to get on top of the gardening chores.

Below
Daffodils are the epitome of spring, but other bulbs, such as these *Ipheion* and *Muscari*, also have their place.

Freshness and light

The flowers at this time of year seem to reflect the pervading mood; they are all full of color and freshness: bright reds, yellows, and blues. Many of them—think of the crocuses or tulips, for example—have shiny petals that reflect the light, adding to the gaiety of the season. The foliage also has a very fresh appeal about it, even on plants as they emerge from below the ground and have yet to flower.

Space fillers

Not many gardeners have enough space to devote a whole border to spring flowers, but it is surprising how many flowers can be packed into borders that mainly flower later in the year. The trick is to take advantage of the fact that most herbaceous material has not yet awakened, and there is plenty of bare earth between the clumps of plants. Bulbs, in particular, can utilize all these spaces.

Daffodils, bluebells, anemones, crocuses, and grape hyacinths can all be planted in the gaps between plants. The only problem is to remember they are there and not stick a fork through them when digging in the border. Spring herbaceous plants take up more space and should be given a permanent position in a border. Some, such as the pulmonarias and bergenias, earn their keep in the summer borders as foliage plants, although they have long finished flowering.

Using pots

If the border is already tightly packed, it is still possible to introduce spring bulbs and other plants. Plant them in pots and then arrange the pots on the border, perhaps behind emerging foliage so that they cannot be seen. Alternatively, sink the pots into the ground so that they are hidden and then remove them after flowering. Once the flowering is over and the foliage has died down, remove the bulbs and store in paper bags until they can be repotted in the autumn. The pots can then be used for something else.

Underplanting

Many of the spring bulbs and herbaceous plants grow under trees and bushes in the wild, and they flower early in the year so that they can take advantage of the light and moisture filtering through the bare branches. By the time the foliage above them opens, blocking the sun and the rain, the plants have flowered and died back below ground to remain dormant until the next spring. This fact can be used to advantage in the garden. Woodland bulbs and other plants can be planted beneath trees and shrubs in soil that will not be used by other plants later in the year. They will show up while there are no leaves on the shrubs, but their ragged remains will be hidden from view later in the season.

Spring work

Spring can be a busy time, especially if you have not made a start in the winter. Finish working through the borders, weeding, splitting up plants, planting new ones, and mulching. As the herbaceous plants emerge, stake those that will need it when they are about a third of their eventual height. Do not delay until the plants fall over as they will never look right. Prune flowering shrubs as they finish blooming and plant annuals once the threat of frost has passed.

Spring bulbs

Anemone blanda Wood anemone
A small woodland bulb covered with white, blue, or pink daisy-like flowers

Chionodoxa
Small bulbs with fresh green foliage and blue or pink flowers

Corydalis
Ferny foliage and flowers in various colors, such as yellow and bright blue

Crocus
Small bulbs with open, cup-shaped blooms in a wide range of colors

Eranthis Winter aconite
A little woodland bulb with golden flowers surrounded by green ruffs

Galanthus Snowdrop
A small early-flowering bulb with white flowers

Leucojum vernum Snowflake
Resembling large snowdrops but flowering later in the season

Narcissus Daffodil
Comes in all shapes and sizes in shades of yellow, orange, and white

Puschkinia
A low-growing spring bulb with blue flowers

Romulea
A very small spring bulb with purplle-pink flowers

Scilla
A small spring bulb with bright blue flowers

Tulipa Tulip
A medium-height bulb with flowers in a wide range of colors

Spring perennials

Aubrieta deltoidea
A well-known rock plant with purple flowers

Bergenia cordifolia Elephant's ears
Forms clumps of leathery leaves and pink or white flowers

Caltha palustris
A low-growing perennial with yellow, cup-shaped flowers

Doronicum 'Miss Mason'
A small-to-medium perennial with bright yellow, daisy-like flowers

Euphorbia polychroma
A small-to-medium perennial with acid green-yellow flowers and bracts

Helleborus orientalis Lenten rose
An evergreen, medium-height perennial with downward-hanging flowers in a variety of colors

Primula vulgaris Primrose
A small perennial forming rosettes of foliage and yellow flowers

Pulmonaria angustifolia
A low-growing plant with vivid blue flowers

Sanguinaria canadensis
An endearing, low-growing plant with white flowers, each enfolded in a leaf

Smilacina racemosa
A medium-height perennial with white flowers

Trollius europaeus
A medium-height perennial with bright yellow-orange, globe-shaped flowers

Viola odorata Violet
A bushy, low-growing plant with violet or white flowers

Early Summer

Early summer is one of the most delightful times in the garden. It still retains much of the freshness of spring, but at the same time it takes on the ebullience and lushness of summer. The borders are beginning to fill with color and the sun is finding its strength.

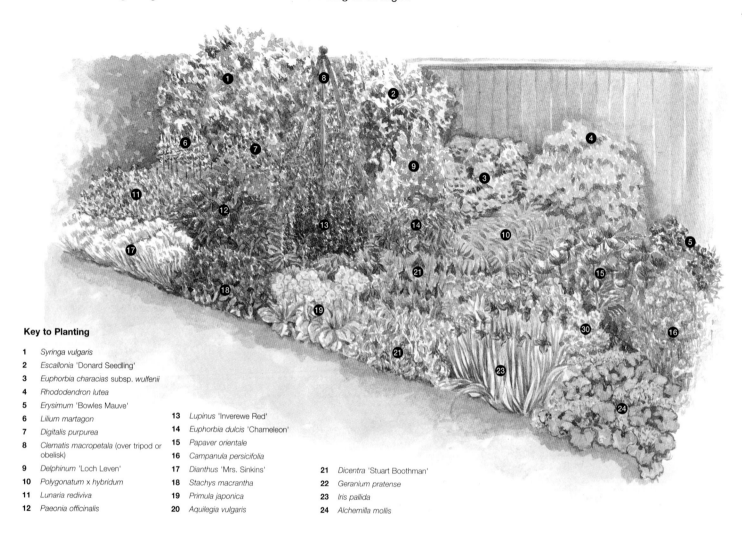

Key to Planting

1 *Syringa vulgaris*
2 *Escallonia 'Donard Seedling'*
3 *Euphorbia characias* subsp. *wulfenii*
4 *Rhododendron lutea*
5 *Erysimum 'Bowles Mauve'*
6 *Lilium martagon*
7 *Digitalis purpurea*
8 *Clematis macropetala* (over tripod or obelisk)
9 *Delphinum 'Loch Leven'*
10 *Polygonatum x hybridum*
11 *Lunaria rediviva*
12 *Paeonia officinalis*

13 *Lupinus 'Inverewe Red'*
14 *Euphorbia dulcis 'Chameleon'*
15 *Papaver orientale*
16 *Campanula persicifolia*
17 *Dianthus 'Mrs. Sinkins'*
18 *Stachys macrantha*
19 *Primula japonica*
20 *Aquilegia vulgaris*

21 *Dicentra 'Stuart Boothman'*
22 *Geranium pratense*
23 *Iris pallida*
24 *Alchemilla mollis*

Early summer colors

The spring is mainly dominated by the primary colors, blue, yellow, and red, but once we move into the summer the palette is extended and a much wider range of colors present themselves. It is a time when carefully thought-out color schemes begin to show whether they have worked or not. For many gardeners it is very difficult to be ruthless, but if you have created a color scheme and something is wrong, dig out the offending plants. For example, if a purple foxglove (*Digitalis purpurea*) appears in the middle of a hot-colored border, then remove it as soon as it shows. It may seem a waste of a plant, but it will be a waste of a border if you leave it, as the whole effect will be ruined. In a bed where precise colors are not important, there is less of a problem. Indeed, self-sown plants often add a touch of spontaneity to a border.

Summer bedding

The late spring and early summer is the time to plant out the tender summer annuals, either as bedding plants in special beds or as part of a mixed border. If there is space it is always a good thing on which to grow the bedding plants, so that they are either near flowering or just flowering as they are planted. This will ensure that they are effective right from the start. Bedding plants added to a mixed border will not only give color in the early summer but continue throughout the summer and into autumn.

Perennials

Apart from a few early spring perennials, such as hellebores and pulmonarias, the transition from late spring to early summer is the beginning of the perennial season. Suddenly all the energy that has rapidly pushed up the green sweels of foliage erupts in a wealth of flowers. No one color dominates at this time of year. It is possible to color-coordinate the borders, but often the freshness and vitality seem somehow to require mixed colors. The colors are offset by the fresh growth of later-flowering perennials. Although the main perennial season is yet to come, for many gardeners this is the most exciting time of year. The weather also reflects this as there is still a freshness in the air.

Trees and shrubs

The spring and early summer are the main flowering times for trees and shrubs. Any later and they would have problems developing seed fast enough to be fully grown before autumn. All the deciduous trees and shrubs are now in full leaf, recently enough still to look fresh. These fill out the border considerably, giving it much more of a three-dimensional look. When planning a bed, it should be remembered just how solid these plants can be and that unless they are low, nothing should be planted behind that is likely to be hidden.

Roses fall into two categories: those that only flower once and those that continue throughout the summer. Most that have just one abundant flowering at this time of year put on a wonderful display.

Early summer work

If all has gone to plan then the beds should be in tiptop condition by now. Keep an eye out for weeds and remove any on sight. Deadheading helps to keep the beds looking fresh. Many spring-flowering shrubs should be pruned now. In dry weather, continue to water any plants planted in the spring until they have become well established.

Early summer perennials

Alchemilla mollis Lady's mantle
A clump-forming plant with handsome foliage and a haze of green-yellow flowers

Baptisia australis
A medium-to-tall perennial with blue flowers

Campanula persicifolia
A medium-height perennial with blue, bell-shaped flowers

Centaurea montana
A low-to-medium perennial with lilac-blue, ragged, daisy-like flowers

Dianthus 'Mrs. Sinkins' Pink
A perennial that produces white flowers above clumps of spiky foliage

Geranium pratense
A medium-height hardy geranium with blue and white flowers

Hemerocallis Daylily
Clumps of medium-height spiky foliage and yellow, orange, or red trumpet-shaped flowers

Iris germanica
A medium-height plant with sword-shaped leaves and flowers in various colors

Lupinus Russell hybrids Lupin
A medium-height perennial with flower spikes in a range of colors

Paeonia officinalis Peony
A medium-height perennial with large red flowers

Papaver orientalis Oriental poppy
A medium-height perennial with huge flowers in red, orange, pink, or white

Stachys macrantha
A low-growing perennial with spikes of pink flowers

Early summer shrubs

Cistus purpureus
A medium shrub with exotic-looking purple flowers

Clematis montana
A vigorous climber literally covered with soft pink flowers

Daphne tangutica
A medium-height shrub with scented pink flowers

Escallonia 'Donnard Seedling'
A tall shrub with many small pink flowers

Lonicera periclymenum Honeysuckle
A climber with pinky-yellow scented blooms

Malus 'John Downie'
A tall shrub with pink flowers, followed by fruits later in the year

Phlomis fruticosa
A medium shrub with yellow flowers and grayish foliage

Potentilla fruticosa
A medium bushy shrub with yellow, pink, or white flowers

Prunus triloba
A small-to-medium shrub with very pretty pink flowers

Rhododendron luteum
A medium shrub with yellow flowers

Rosa 'Madame Grégoire Staechelin'
A climbing rose covered with pink flowers in early summer

Syringa vulgaris Lilac
A tall shrub with scented lilac or white flowers

Left These aquilegias and geraniums provide delicate notes of fresh early-summer color.

Mid-to-Late Summer

Mid-to-late summer is the highlight of the gardening year but at the same time there is the hint of the decline to come. Many plants have finished flowering and the foliage is beginning to look tired. However, with judicious removal of dead and dying plants, the borders can be kept very much alive with a continuing display of color and texture.

Summer colors

During mid- and late summer there is a complete range of colors for the gardener's palette. The colors are perhaps not as sparkling fresh as in the spring, and the strong summer sun has a tendency to flatten them, but there is still plenty of scope for creating a very pleasing garden. At this the time of year color themes are at their best. White schemes, in particular, retain their freshness and tranquillity. Blue and yellow also add a touch of freshness to the summer scene.

Annuals and bedding

Many annuals and bedding plants will continue to flower through the summer. The plants grow to fill the available space and often beyond. Remove straggly stems and cut back dying flowers so they remain fresh. It is useful to keep a few spares growing in pots to slot into gaps in the border. From time to time plants will die or leave an ugly gap once they have been cut back, and a few annuals can quickly repair the damage.

Perennials

Perennials are at their best at this time of year. However, unless those that have finished flowering have been deadheaded and any flagging foliage removed, the border can look ragged. Cut back plants such as *Alchemilla* *mollis* and a number of the geraniums to the ground to tidy the borders and stimulate the plants into producing fresh new foliage. If the old leaves and stems are left, they will look increasingly ragged and considerably spoil the overall effect of the border.

Below
As the weather gets warmer and the summer progresses, the hotter colors come into their own.

Mid-to-late summer perennials

Acanthus spinosus
A medium-tall plant with handsome glossy leaves and purple and white flowers

Aster x frikartii
A medium-height perennial with blue daisy-like flowers

Catananche caerulea
A low-growing perennial with blue daisy-like flowers

Dianthus 'Doris' Pink
A low-growing plant with pink flowers over spiky foliage

Geranium 'Patricia'
A low-growing hardy geranium with magenta flowers

Helenium 'Moerheim Beauty'
A medium-to-tall perennial with orange-brown flowers

Hemerocallis 'Stafford' Daylily
A medium-height plant forming clumps of spiky foliage and mahogany flowers

Kniphofia 'Little Maid'
A low-to-medium perennial with spiky foliage and cream flowers

Leucanthemum superbum
A medium plant with white daisy-like flowers

Macleaya cordata
A tall perennial with spikes of coral flowers

Monarda 'Croftway Pink' Bergamot
A medium-height plant with shaggy pink flowers

Penstemon 'Andenken an Friedrich Hahn'
A medium-height perennial with red flowers

Late summer shrubs

Abutilon 'Kentish Belle'
A medium shrub with large yellow flowers

Buddleja davidii Butterfly bush
A tall shrub with mauve flowers

Caryopteris x clandonensis
A low shrub with rich blue flowers and grayish foliage

Clematis 'Perle d'Azur'
A climber with blue flowers

Deutzia x elegantissima 'Rosealind'
A medium shrub with very pretty pink flowers

Fuchsia magellanica
A medium hardy fuchsia with red flowers

Hebe salicifolia
A medium-to-tall shrub covered with spikes of white flowers

Hydrangea macrophylla
A medium, rounded shrub with blue or pink flowers

Hypericum x inodorum 'Elstead'
A medium shrub with yellow flowers

Indigofera heterantha
A medium-to-tall shrub with pink flowers

Lavandula angustifolia Lavender
A low-growing shrub with spikes of lavender flowers

Rosa 'New Dawn'
A pink-flowered climbing rose

Trees and shrubs

The trees and shrubs will continue to create a permanent feature in the border as all else changes around them. However, they are now in their most boring phase as most have finished flowering and by the end of the season their foliage is beginning to look rather tired. One way of pepping them up is to grow late-flowering clematis, such as the viticellas, up through them. These are cut back almost to the ground in the winter, so they do not interfere with the appearance of the shrub when it is in flower in the early part of the season.

Mid-to-late summer work

Summer is the time to relax and really enjoy the garden. There are still things to do, but this is mainly restricted to removing any weeds that dare show their face, and to deadheading and removing other dead or dying material. Avoid planting new material at this time of year as it is usually too hot and dry for the plants to get established.

Autumn

Autumn is quitting time in the garden. More and more plants finish flowering and start to retire back below the ground. However, there are a remarkable number of plants that will go on flowering until the first frosts and often beyond. It is important to seek these out and include them in the borders so that the interest is kept going as long as possible.

Autumn color

The flowers of autumn have a very distinct feel. In many ways they are the same colors as spring, but now instead of bright fresh yellows, we have the more somber golds. The colors now have a richness about them: the purples are deep purples and the yellows deep yellows. There is still sparkle but it often needs the sun to bring it out. The leaves take on a darker tone as they begin to age. Many eventually develop wonderful autumn tints as they prepare to drop.

Annuals and bedding

There are few annuals or bedding plants that are specifically for the autumn. In the wild most would have to be in seed by now or their succession would not be assured. In the garden, however, many of those that were planted out in the late spring are still flowering. Many are likely to have gotten very lax and leggy. Trimming them back will prolong their useful life and promote fresh flowers by keeping them neat and tidy.

Perennials

Many perennials, such as the penstemons, will continue from the summer well into the autumn. There are also a surprising number of plants that flower only in the autumn and it is worth making certain that a number of these are included in the border. Asters like Michaelmas daisies are particularly good.

It is very important to remove any flagging plants as they die back. This will not only make the border look tidier but will also allow the autumn-flowering plants to be seen clearly. There are a few autumn-flowering bulbs, such as colchicums, nerines, and amaryllis, which can be planted between plants that have finished so that they fill the gaps.

Below
There is no mistaking the rich autumn colors. Their arrival is a definite signal that the year is winding down.

Trees and shrubs

While most perennials and annuals disappear
with no more than a whimper, many trees and
shrubs go out in a blaze of glory. Their foliage
can be fantastic. However, it should be placed
well if used in a border because it must fit in
with any plants that are still in flower. Another
aspect to remember is that many also have
fruits or berries which will add to the attraction
of the border at a time when most things are
rapidly fading. These are not only attractive to
look at but also provide food for birds and other
animals.

Autumn work

Continue to clean up, removing all dead material
as it goes over. Some gardeners like to leave
some of the more attractive seed heads as
winter decoration in the borders. These also
help to provide birds with food in the winter
months. Autumn is also a good time for
preparing new borders, digging them over and
leaving them to weather over the winter.

Autumn flowers

Amaryllis belladonna
A medium-height bulb with pink, trumpet-
shaped flowers

***Anemone hybrida* Japanese anemone**
A medium perennial with pink flowers

***Aster novae-angliae* 'Harrington's Pink'**
A tall perennial with pink daisy-like flowers

Colchicum speciosum
A low-growing bulb with showy pink flowers

Helianthus salicifolius
A tall perennial with yellow daisy-like flowers

Leucanthemella serotina
A tall-growing perennial with white flowers

Liriope muscari
A low-growing perennial with grassy foliage
and spikes of blue-purple flowers

Nerine bowdenii
A low-growing bulb with pink, trumpet-
shaped flowers

Rudbeckia hirta
A low to medium-growing perennial with
golden daisy-like flowers

Schizostylis coccinea
A medium-height bulb with spikes of
elegant pink flowers

***Sedum* Herbstfreude**
A fleshy, medium-height perennial with large
clumps of pink flowers

Vernonia crinita
A tall perennial with purple flowers

Autumn foliage color

***Acer palmatum* Japanese maple**
A large shrub or small tree that turns red,
orange, or yellow

Amelanchier lamarckii
A large shrub that turns red and orange

Berberis thunbergii
A medium shrub with red-orange autumn
tints

Betula utilis
A small tree with tiny leaves that turn yellow

Ceratostigma willmottianum
A low-growing shrub that turns bright red

***Cotinus* 'Flame' Smoke bush**
A medium-tall shrub that turns a shocking
red

Enkianthus campanulatus
A medium-to-tall shrub taking on bright red
autumn tints

Euonymus alatus
A medium, dense shrub with red autumn
color

Fothergilla major
A medium shrub with red, orange, and
yellow autumn foliage

Rhododendron luteum
A medium-height azalea with rich autumn
tints

Stephanandra incisa
A low-to-medium, arching shrub with
orange-yellow autumn color

Viburnum opulus
A medium-to-tall shrub with rich red leaves
in autumn

Winter

Winter, in theory, is a time to rest for both the garden and the gardener, but it rarely is. A great deal of activity is taking place below ground as plants start into growth. Above ground there are a surprising number of plants that take the opportunity to flower while there is little competition around. It is also a time when the gardener will benefit from working in the garden if conditions allow.

Below
Winter in the garden depends on quite different elements than the rest of the year. The bare bones of the garden provide the interest.

Winter flowers

A surprising number of plants flower in the winter. Many of these are shrubs, but there are also perennials and bulbs. A large number of these are scented, often highly so. The reason for this is that pollinating insects are few and far between in the winter so the flowers must do everything possible to attract them. Those that are unscented are mainly wind pollinated. Most seem to be resilient to weather and need no protection from it; they may bow their heads in a frost, but soon come up again.

Winter stems

There are a number of trees and shrubs that have attractive bark, which shows up to its best advantage in winter when there is little else to obscure it. However, it is difficult to justify these in a border in a small garden, as perhaps the space would be better used for plants that are at their best when the garden is most in use. In a bigger garden, though, they are well worth growing.

Another aspect of winter stems is that the dead stems of many grasses and herbaceous plants are very attractive. If left standing for at least part of the winter they will create an interesting picture, especially when viewed from indoors on a frosty or snowy day.

Winter borders

Rather than have winter-flowering or winter-interest plants scattered around the garden, some gardeners like to create a winter border where they bring together not only all those plants that flower but also those with colored or otherwise attractive bark, plus interesting evergreens. This works very well if you have plenty of space, but it is difficult to justify if space is small.

The more usual place to grow winter-flowering plants is in the general borders. Since many of these plants are dull or even bedraggled during the summer, it is a good idea to plant them at the back of the border or elsewhere, where they are masked by herbaceous plants during the summer months. This allows them to show up in the winter when everything else is either below ground or at least out of leaf, but be covered up and out of sight during the summer.

Winter work

An hour spent working on a border in winter will save several hours of work later in the year. If the weather is fine and the soil not too damp, then the more work done the better. However, it is important not to work on waterlogged beds or the soil structure will be destroyed. If you are uncertain, work from the path or from planks of wood without getting on the soil. Dig between the plants, weed, and mulch. Remove all dead material from last year's plants and any dead or damaged material from trees and shrubs.

Below
The stems of trees and shrubs, rather than the foliage, produce much of the color in the winter garden.

Winter-flowering plants

Cornus mas
A medium or large shrub with yellow flowers

Daphne mezereum
A medium-height shrub with wonderfully scented pink flowers

Eranthis hyemalis Winter aconite
A pretty little bulb with yellow, cup-shaped flowers

Galanthus nivalis Snowdrop
A small bulb with pendulous white flowers

Helleborus niger Christmas rose
A low-growing perennial with flat, open white flowers

Iris unguicularis
A handsome perennial with a fan of sword-shaped leaves and mauve flowers

Jasminum nudiflorum Winter jasmine
A wiry shrub with yellow flowers

Lonicera fragrantissima
A medium-to-tall shrub with scented pale yellow flowers on the bare stems

Mahonia x media 'Charity'
A medium-to-tall evergreen shrub with sprays of scented yellow flowers

Sarcococca confusa
A small-to-medium evergreen shrub with scented white flowers

Viburnum bodnantense
A medium-sized shrub with scented pink flowers

Viola odorata Violet
A carpeting perennial with little violet flowers

Attractive winter bark

Acer griseum Paper bark maple
A tree with peeling, russet bark

Acer davidii Snake bark maple
A tall tree with striped, snake-like bark

Betulus utilis jacquemontii Birch
A tree with wonderful silver bark

Cornus alba 'Sibirica' Red dogwood
A vigorous shrub with scarlet stems

Corylus avellana 'Contorta' Twisted hazel
A tree with curved and twisted branches

Eucalyptus gunnii
A very tall tree with smooth, patchy bark

Euonymus alatus
A medium shrub with bright autumn color and interesting winter bark

Prunus serrula
A tall tree with shiny mahogany bark

Rubus cockburnianus
A medium shrub forming a thicket of ghostly white stems

Rubus thibetanus
A medium shrub with white-bloomed brown stems

Salix alba subsp. **vitellina**
A medium shrub with yellow shoots in winter

Salix alba subsp. **vitellina 'Britzensis'**
A medium shrub with bright orange-red new shoots

Borders for Special Conditions

While most borders are suitable for most gardens, either big or small, there are certain conditions that need special borders and particular plants that will thrive there. These include shady areas, very hot and dry areas, and wet areas in the garden.

There is nothing difficult about this, the secret is to use plants that naturally grow in these special conditions. Thus if you try to grow sun-loving plants in the shade, you are doomed to failure, but if you grow woodland plants there then success is much more likely. In some cases you can change conditions. For example, shade can be removed by cutting down or thinning trees and shrubs; wet ground can be drained. If the whole garden is covered by this condition then it would be a good thing to alter at least part of it. However, a garden with different types of habitat is a much more exciting place. Soil types are notoriously difficult to change, but it is possible at least to adapt them a little to broaden the spectrum of plants that can be grown there.

On the other hand, of course, you may actually want to create these conditions. In a sunny garden there is nowhere to grow shade-loving plants, which is a great loss. And likewise, most gardens benefit from having water and associated borders somewhere in them.

As well as borders that relate to special garden conditions, there are those that relate to the gardener's own personal position. There are many people who, for physical reasons such as age or infirmity, are not able to garden in the conventional way. There are special types of borders that can be constructed, perhaps with some initial help, that will enable them to continue to enjoy their gardening and garden.

Special borders do not necessarily involve any more work than ordinary borders, although it may be different. There are certainly no special skills that any gardener should not be competent to carry out. As always, the key is thorough preparation before you start, especially by removing all perennial weeds.

Shade

Shade is regarded by many gardeners as a problem. In fact, it should be seen as a blessing as it allows the gardener to grow a whole range of plants that he or she would not otherwise be able to try. While perhaps not as colorful as many of the sun-lovers, there are still plenty of attractive and intriguing plants that will create a border full of interest.

The key to success

The key to growing plants in the shade is to choose species that naturally grow in these conditions. Any attempt to grow plants that normally like sun will be unsuccessful, as they will not like the conditions and will turn out to be miserable specimens that eventually die. This rules out a lot of bedding plants and most of those with silver foliage.

Woodlanders

Most plants that grow in the shade in the wild are woodlanders, or at least grow under trees and shrubs. These are, naturally, the best plants to grow in the shade. A vast number of these are in cultivation from all round the world. Plants that grow in the spring predominate but there are also some for all the other seasons, including winter.

Many woodland plants emerge, flower, set seed and die back below ground in the late winter and early spring while the deciduous trees and shrubs are without leaves, allowing light and rain to get to the plants. It is a good idea to position these in the garden under deciduous plants, so the bare patch they leave through the rest of the year will be covered by the foliage of the plant above.

Left

Shade should not be seen as a problem but as a benefit, providing a different type of habitat in which to grow interesting plants.

Foliage effect

In woodland areas, it is not always the flowers that create the effect but often foliage of different shapes and shades of green. There are a number of plants that will help create this effect, including hostas, ferns and, of course, many trees and shrubs. Few grasses will grow in such conditions.

Bedding borders

It is not very easy to grow bedding in a shady position. There are a few bedding plants that will tolerate light shade and should grow, for example, in a border near a shady wall where there is light but no sun. Impatiens, tobacco plants (*Nicotiana*), and pansies (*Viola wittrockiana*) will grow in these conditions. However, it is not really possible to create large-scale bedding designs in shade in the same way as it is in the open.

Creating shade borders

Shade borders can be built where shade is caused by buildings, tall walls, or fences. They can also be created in the shade of trees or shrubs. This need not be a full-scale wood; even one shrub is sufficient to provide enough shade for growing at least a few shade-loving plants. Most woodland soils have a lot of leaf mold in them and this is very much to the liking of most shade-loving plants. Try to emulate such a soil by adding as much well-rotted organic material to the soil as you can, especially leaf mold if you have it.

Letting in light

There are few plants that like growing in very dense shade, especially when the soil is dry; so avoid planting under yew, for example. Trees and shrubs that sweep right to the ground also present problems. However, it is often possible to thin out a few branches or remove the lower ones so that more light enters your chosen area. This will improve the conditions and widen the selection of plants that will grow there.

Below

A wide variety of attractive shade-loving plants can be used under trees. Avoid using sun-lovers.

Flowers for shade

Anemone nemorosa Wood anemone
A low-growing plant with white flowers in spring

Brunnera macrophylla
A low-growing perennial with bright blue flowers in spring

Convallaria majalis Lily of the Valley
A spreading perennial with scented white flowers in late spring to summer

Eranthis hyemalis Winter aconite
A tiny yellow-flowered bulb, blooming in late winter to spring

Euphorbia amygdaloides var. *robbiae*
A medium-height perennial with acid-green flowers in spring

Helleborus viridis
A low to medium-height perennial with green flowers in winter to spring

Lamium galeobdolon Yellow deadnettle
A low-growing, spreading perennial with yellow flowers in spring

Lathyrus vernus
A perennial sweet pea with purple flowers in spring to summer

Liriope muscari
A low-growing perennial with spikes of blue-purple flowers in autumn

Sanguinaria canadensis
A low-growing, spring-flowering perennial with white flowers

Smilacina racemosa
A medium-height perennial with white flowers in early summer

Trillium grandiflorum Wake robin
A low-growing perennial with white flowers in late spring or early summer

Hot and Dry Areas

There has been a great revival of interest in growing plants in Mediterranean conditions—that is, hot and dry for most of the summer, with just occasional downpours of rain. While it is not possible to create the climatic conditions, it is possible to simulate the physical conditions. The resulting border can be quite stunning and very different from conventional herbaceous and mixed borders.

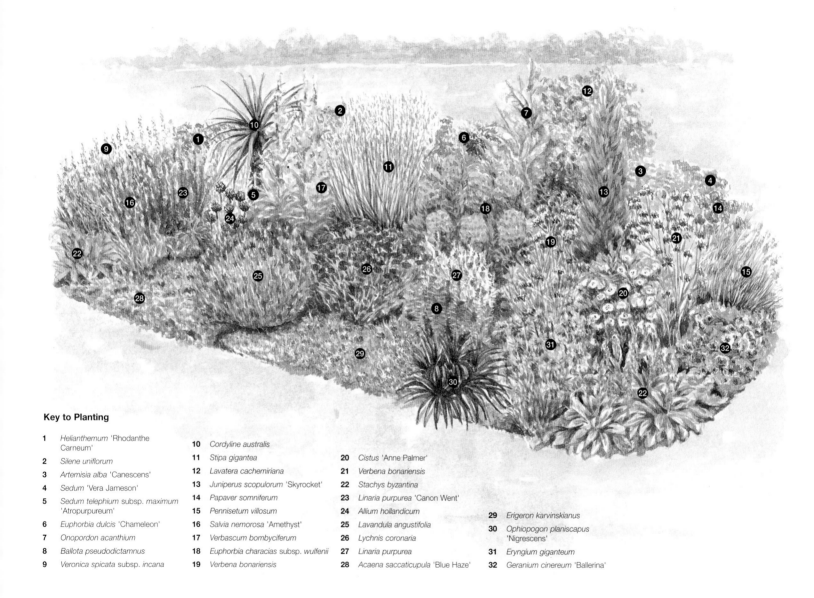

Key to Planting

1	Helianthemum 'Rhodanthe Carneum'	10	Cordyline australis	20	Cistus 'Anne Palmer'
2	Silene uniflorum	11	Stipa gigantea	21	Verbena bonariensis
3	Artemisia alba 'Canescens'	12	Lavatera cachemiriana	22	Stachys byzantina
4	Sedum 'Vera Jameson'	13	Juniperus scopulorum 'Skyrocket'	23	Linaria purpurea 'Canon Went'
5	Sedum telephium subsp. maximum 'Atropurpureum'	14	Papaver somniferum	24	Allium hollandicum
		15	Pennisetum villosum	25	Lavandula angustifolia
6	Euphorbia dulcis 'Chameleon'	16	Salvia nemorosa 'Amethyst'	26	Lychnis coronaria
7	Onopordon acanthium	17	Verbascum bombyciferum	27	Linaria purpurea
8	Ballota pseudodictamnus	18	Euphorbia characias subsp. wulfenii	28	Acaena saccaticupula 'Blue Haze'
9	Veronica spicata subsp. incana	19	Verbena bonariensis		

29	Erigeron karvinskianus
30	Ophiopogon planiscapus 'Nigrescens'
31	Eryngium giganteum
32	Geranium cinereum 'Ballerina'

Dry conditions

Although a mainly dry and sunny climate is desirable for a Mediterranean border, it is not essential. What is essential, however, is a free-draining soil that will prevent any stagnant water settling around the plants' roots. Although the soil should be free-draining, it should only remove excess water. The soil should include sufficient humus to hold enough moisture for the plants' use. In the wild this is likely to be detritus and old plant material. In the garden it can be any well-rotted organic material as long as it is not too rich in nitrogen, as most of these plants are not heavy feeders.

Creating a Mediterranean border

Such a border should be in an open position, where there is plenty of sun and circulating air. It should not be enclosed and humid. Ordinary garden soil can be used as a basis as long as it is not too heavy. First dig over the soil in the autumn, removing any perennial weeds. In the spring dig through it again, removing any weeds that have regenerated and this time incorporating some leaf mold and plenty of coarse sand or gravel. The leaf mold will help to retain sufficient moisture, while the gravel will help the excess to drain away.

In heavier soils, digging such a bed is likely to create a sump, with water collecting in it rather than draining away. In these conditions it is essential to lay drains of some sort to remove any water that is likely to lie in the bed. A heavy soil will take a lot of breaking down. Grit, gravel, or sand are the best for this. However, this still may not improve the situation, and it may be best either to import a load of quality topsoil and replace the heavy clay with it, or to build a raised bed, again with good topsoil so that the bed is above the heavy ground and will drain onto it. The resulting bed should be such that if you throw a bucket of water on it, it immediately seeps away and does not leave puddles.

The plants

There is a wide range of plants that like such situations. Many of them, naturally, come from Mediterranean regions. There are also other plants that are found in colder areas but which grow in well-drained situations, along gravelly seashores, for example, or in sandy soils.

Most of the plants with silver or gray foliage do well in a Mediterranean border. Many bulbs also enjoy these conditions, especially plants such as alliums.

Final appearance

Once the plants have been planted, it is a good idea to top dress the whole bed with gravel or small stones. These will not only create an appropriate background against which to see the plants but will also help to improve the growing conditions, by providing a mulch to keep weeds down. It also ensures that there is a very well-drained "collar" around each plant at a point that is very vulnerable to rotting-off in damp conditions.

A Mediterranean bed can be a simple, flat affair or it can be undulated to make the surface more interesting. The plants are not planted as close together as they are in a normal bed, partly so that plants have adequate moisture and nutrients and partly to allow plenty of air to circulate between them. This space means that the appearance of the surface is important. An interesting design is to create a dry river course, decorating the "river" with larger stones and weather-worn pieces of wood or driftwood in intriguing shapes.

Below
Succulent plants such as these agaves, kalanchoes, and sedums are very good for growing in hot, dry soils.

Waterside Areas

Most gardens benefit from some form of water feature, even if it is only a waterspout trickling into a basin. This is partly because of the tranquil atmosphere that water creates, but also because it extends the number of plants you can grow. The plants may be grown in the water itself or in a moist, boggy bed beside the pond. Because of the ready supply of moisture, such beds often have a fresh colorful appearance, even in midsummer, which is quite different from other borders.

Right
Water features are often under-planted, with too much of the surrounding rockwork exposed, Here the balance is just right.

The plants

Borders beside water can have a wide range of plants in them. They vary from the marginals, which grow in the mud on the edge of the pond, often in the shallow water, through those that grow in the boggy edge of the pond, to those that grow on comparatively dry ground. In a wider view, they can also include those plants that actually grow in the pond, such as waterlilies.

In the pond

Those plants in the deeper water can be grown in the mud at the bottom of the pond if it is a natural one, but in the more likely event that it is lined, in special plastic baskets. These can be filled with a special pond compost or ordinary compost and covered with a thick layer of gravel so that the lighter material in the compost does not float away.

On the margins

There are a number of plants that do not mind growing in shallow water. These are useful as they help to soften the junction between the pond and the shore, and hide the liner if it is showing. Plants such as *Iris laevigata* and *Caltha palustris* are ideal. Again, if the pond is natural they can be planted directly in the mud or even the bank. A lined pond should be constructed in such a way that there are stepped ledges leading to the deeper water on which lattice pots or baskets can be placed.

Left
Plants in bog gardens grow lushly and vigorously, putting on a wonderful display of flowers and foliage.

The bog garden

The border next to the pond is the bog garden. This comprises plants that like to grow in moist conditions, but not in standing water. There are a large number of these, many of them either colorful or with interesting, often large foliage. The important thing about a bog garden is that it must be kept moist. If a pond is lined either with plastic membrane or with clay, the area beyond it will be dry (after all, the purpose of the liner is to keep the water in). Therefore, arrangements must be made to allow a certain amount of water to seep into the bed, perhaps by lowering the liner at one point so that every time the pond is refilled it overflows into this area.

The best way of creating a bed in normal soil is to excavate a shallow depression and line it with polythene or an old pond liner. Puncture the bottom in a few places to let excess water drain away. Fill with a mixture of soil and humus. Such a bed need not have a pond associated with it as long as it is watered regularly.

Streamside borders

A similar border to a bog garden can be built along the side of a stream. If the stream is lined with cement or a pond liner, again, moisture will not get into the bed. However, if there are waterfalls, inevitably water will splash onto the banks and here small colonies of moisture-loving plants can be planted. This type of grouping has a natural look to it.

Waterside perennials

Aruncus dioicus
A medium-to-tall plant with cream flowers in summer

Astilbe x arendsii
A low-to-medium-growing plant with feathery foliage and cream, pink, or purple flower spikes in summer

Caltha palustris
A low-growing plant with yellow cup-shaped flowers in spring

Cardamine pratensis
A low-growing perennial with lilac spring flowers

Gunnera manicata
An enormous foliage plant with immense leaves

Iris ensata
A medium-height water iris with blue flowers in summer

Lobelia cardinalis
A medium-height plant producing spikes of scarlet flowers in summer

Lythrum salicaria
A medium-height perennial with purple flowers in late summer

Onoclea sensibilis
A handsome, medium-height fern with divided foliage

Persicaria bistorta
A vigorous, low-growing perennial with pink flowers in summer

Primula japonica
A rosette-forming perennial with pink or white candelabra flowers in summer

Rodgersia pinnata
A medium-to-tall perennial with architectural foliage and cream-pink flowers in summer

Elderly and Disabled Gardeners

As we grow older it is not always possible to achieve all the things we have formerly done; although the mind is willing, the body is not always capable of keeping up with our desires. This can be devastating after a lifetime of gardening. There are also those who, through accident or disability, cannot achieve as much as they would like. Fortunately, there are some measures that can be taken to help at least some of these people to garden. As a general rule, elderly gardeners should consider gradually turning over their borders to more low-maintenance ones (see page 21) as well as converting them to more manageable heights.

Tools and equipment

There is now a wide range of specialized tools for the disabled and elderly. These are mainly specially developed so that they are easier to hold. Others have special mechanisms built into them to facilitate their operation. For example, there are spring-loaded spades which turn the soil with out the necessity to bend down and pick up the spade full of earth. Some larger stores carry these tools, and there are several mail-order firms with catalogs.

Raising the height

Along with problems of holding and handling tools, there is the problem of bending: the ground can seem a long way away when you want to remove a weed. One way of coping with this is to bring the ground up to a reasonable level so that it can be attended without bending or from a wheelchair.

The way to do this is by building your borders in raised beds. These are brick, concrete-block, or wooden structures filled with soil. They should not be too wide, just wide enough so that all parts of the bed can be reached without overstretching. The height of the bed should vary according to the person using it; a bed for a wheelchair will be lower than one for somebody standing. The depth of soil will depend on what

Right
Plants can be brought up to a more manageable level in raised beds or, as here, in naturalistic settings.

you want to grow; alpines will grow in a shallower soil than, say, herbaceous plants.

For wheelchair use the bed can be in the form of a tray raised on pillars so that the lower part of the chair will fit under the tray, allowing the person to get right up to bed. Any such structure should be absolutely stable with no chance that the whole thing could topple. Avoid balancing boxes of soil on top of a pile of bricks—either build it or get it built properly.

Fragrant borders

For those with poor sight or hearing, smell and touch become more important senses than for those with good sight. For them a border of scented flowers can be a great joy. A narrow bed with tactile plants, such as soft grasses, or velvety or coarse leaves, will also increase the

range of plants that can be appreciated. Place a seat next to the border for maximum enjoyment.

Getting about

Not all ground is level because of either the slope or the unevenness of the path. Try to make certain that the approaches to borders and paths around them are even, without anything to trip over. Create shallow ramps between different areas rather than steps. This will not only make walking between the areas easier, but will allow wheelchairs to be moved freely about the garden. In areas where the ground is terraced, provide railings both for support and to prevent falls. These are also important for steps and ramps. It is always a good thing to provide plenty of seating, as elderly people often like to rest as well as to sit and appreciate the borders.

Above

Allium schoenoprasum and *Phuopsis stylosa* both have spherical pink flowers and curious fragrances, the former onion-like and the latter a musty "foxy" smell.

Borders for Special Subjects

In a small garden, a general border containing a wide range of plants that the owner likes is possibly the best use of space. However, there are many reasons for creating a border. Among these is the desire to create something that reflects your personal interests. This may be one particular type of plant, such as the rose, or those that support wildlife or even provide vegetables for the kitchen.

One of the great attractions of owning a garden is the opportunity it gives for conversation. There are few things more pleasurable than strolling around a garden talking about it to a like-minded friend. Creating a specialized area adds greatly to that pleasure. Even nongardening friends seem to find such a border fascinating.

Some towns have only one or two garden centers or nurseries, and it is from these that the majority of plants grown in neighboring gardens are purchased. This does tend to create a certain uniformity or predictability. However, if you set out to create a specialized border, you will have to hunt out the plants that suit it. This in itself is pleasurable and always gives some purpose to looking round nurseries or at catalogs. It also provides the garden with many different and even unusual or rare plants.

One of the great thrills of gardening is suddenly to discover a plant for which you have been searching for years. Collecting plants for a border enhances visits to other gardens and to nurseries; it not only tunes your eye to your own special interest, but also helps you notice other plants. In some cases there are speciality clubs or groups where you have the chance to meet other like-minded growers, swapping not only plants but information and experience.

So specialized borders are created with a secondary purpose in mind. For example, a flower arranger might well create a border devoted to plants that can be cut for either fresh or dried arrangements. Similarly, keen cooks may want to grow their own vegetables. There is no need for borders of this type to be unattractive; as much care can go into the layout as with any other type of border.

Plant Collections

Sooner or later most gardeners become particularly attracted to one group of plants or another. It may be a mild love affair with, say, a few extra geraniums added to a border, or it might lead to the entire garden being turned over to their particular subject. The majority fall somewhere in between and may devote a border to their interest.

Roses

The most common subject of single-plant borders must be roses. Even the humblest garden may contain one or more borders that have little in them other than roses. There is a vast number of roses from which to choose, but choose you must, as the complete range is beyond any one gardener. You can include a mixture of types of roses or you can stick to one type. Old-fashioned or scented roses are popular choices; although others like to collect hybrid teas. To create an interesting border, choose a selection that will give a well-balanced structure to the bed. Choose some climbers to grow over frames or trelliswork, some large shrubs, and some more tightly controlled teas. Standards and miniatures would complete the three-dimensional picture.

Underplanting

The problem with a one-flower border is that there are times when nothing is happening. Some varieties of roses, for example, flower once, usually in early summer, and then they are finished for the year. Others continue to flower throughout the summer and into the autumn or have a single second bloom later in the year. Out of flower, most rose bushes are not the most attractive of plants and it is a good idea to provide some alternative interest to cover this period. One way is to underplant with a different category of plants. Hardy geraniums, for example, go very well with roses and do not conflict with them when the latter are in flower. Primulas or violas make good spring plants that flower before the roses are in bloom.

Below
Violas are very attractive subjects for a collection. There are many varieties and new ones are constantly being created or discovered.

Other subjects

There are plenty of other plants that people collect and for which they create special borders. Many perennials, such as hostas, geraniums, and euphorbias, make perfect subjects. Plants such as these usually look best if mixed with other types of plants. Some, however, such as irises, often do better in their own border.

Growing for show

Sooner or later specialty growers are likely to start showing their plants. This can be great fun, as you not only gain skill in growing plants to a high standard but you will also get to meet a lot of like-minded people. Delphiniums, chrysanthemums, dahlias, sweet peas and roses are some of the most popular subjects. Special borders devoted to these are certainly required for growing show specimens. They need plenty of space between plants so that they can be given the best attention. However, from a visual point of view, borders of this type can be rather boring, so try to include a few other borders of general interest.

More attention

One problem with single-plant borders is that if a pest or a disease gets hold, they can sweep right through the lot, leaving a rather forlorn sight. For example, if you have a rose border and blackspot or greenfly appear, they could devastate the whole border unless action is promptly taken. A mixed border is nowhere near so vulnerable. In such a diversity of plants there will always be some that are not attacked and so will cover for those that are suffering. Also, a mixed border provides a better shelter for insect predators, which will help to reduce the risk of pest attack.

Wildlife

For many people, the only daily contact that they have with nature is through their garden, as they live some distance from the open countryside. For them the birds and other wildlife that appear in the garden are a constant source of joy. By increasing the chances of animals coming to the garden, gardeners will not only enhance their own pleasure but also help to provide habitats for wildlife that is increasingly feeling the pressures of man's encroachment.

Below
Seed heads provide a valuable source of food for birds, relieving the autumn and winter months.

Food

Plants are a source of food to a large percentage of the world's animals. In the garden a border may well provide food for birds, insects and small mammals. This food is generally in the form of fruits and seeds. Growing plants that have suitable berries and seeds for birds is an obvious way of attracting them. Leaving old seed heads on plants through the winter will not only provide food for seed-eaters, but also give places to hide for insects, which in turn are eaten by certain types of birds. There is a sufficiently large range of such plants that the visual attractiveness of the border is not compromised.

Nectar

Plants that have flowers rich in nectar are much loved by butterflies and bees. Mixing at least a few of these into a border will ensure that these delightful insects are always present. Butterflies flitting from flower to flower and bees drowsily droning are two effects that create a sense of well-being in the garden.

Water

Water is useful in the garden as it provides access to water for birds and mammals, not only for drinking but also for washing. Allow some of the banks of a pond to slope gently into the water as this will provide access even if the water level drops. It will also allow any mammals that accidentally fall into the water to find their way out, something they sadly often fail to do in steep-sided ponds.

Water also provides a habitat for dragonflies and the like. Plants growing in and overhanging the water are a favorite resting place for dragonflies, as well as somewhere to lay their eggs.

Home

Shrubs with a compact and branching habit make ideal nesting places for birds. It is a good idea to grow a few in the borders, especially as nesting sites are restricted if you have fences rather than hedges. Thick climbers growing over fences and walls also provide a wealth of possible sites. In the woodland border there is also space for placing a few artificial nesting sites in the form of nest boxes. These should be positioned well above the ground.

Keeping them at bay

Birds and animals are not appreciated in all borders—fruit and vegetable borders, for example. Here the wildlife competes with the gardener for the produce. The best way of coping with this is to erect a fruit cage over the border involved. However, keep the top netting on only when there are crops to protect. Leaving it off at other times will allow birds to forage for pests, especially insects which might otherwise cause damage to the plants. It will also allow freer access for pollinating bees.

Below

Sedum 'Herbstfreude' attracts butterflies in autumn, and the rose provides hips for small mammals and birds when other foods run out.

Plants supplying bird food

Corylus avellana Hazel
A large shrub that produces nuts

Cotoneaster horizontalis
A spreading shrub with red berries

Cynara cardunculus Cardoon
A large perennial with seed heads

Dipsacus fullonum
A biennial with seed heads for birds

Echinops ritro
A perennial with good seed heads

Hedera helix Ivy
A climber with berries

Ilex aquifolium Holly
A shrub or tree with berries

Lonicera periclymenum Honeysuckle
Provides berries and dense growth for nesting

Pyracantha coccinea Firethorn
A shrub with prolific red or orange berries

Sorbus aucuparia Mountain ash
A tree providing berries

Taxus baccata Yew
A shrub or tree providing berries and nesting sites

Viburnum opulus Guelder rose
A large shrub with red berries

Butterfly and bee plants

Aster novae-angliae Michaelmas daisy
A medium-height perennial with daisy-like flowers in late summer to autumn

Buddleja davidii Butterfly bush
A large shrub with purple flowers in summer to autumn

Cephalaria gigantea
A large perennial with yellow flowers in summer

Echinacea purpurea
A medium-height perennial with large purple daisy-like flowers in summer to autumn

Escallonia 'Donard Seedling'
A medium to large shrub that flowers in summer

Hebe salicifolia
A large evergreen shrub with white flowers in summer

Hedera helix Ivy
An evergreen climber with flowers in summer to autumn

Mentha spicata Mint
A medium perennial with lilac flowers in summer

Nepeta x faassenii Catmint
A low-growing perennial with blue-lilac flowers in summer

Scabiosa caucasica
A medium perennial with pincushion flowers in summer

Solidago virgaurea
A medium-height perennial with flowers in late summer to autumn

Thymus serpyllum Thyme
A small shrub with pink-lilac flowers in summer

Wildflowers

Borders containing wildflowers have become popular for two main reasons. The first is simply that the flowers are so attractive. The other is conservation. Man's demands are putting an ever-increasing pressure on the countryside, and the wildflower population in most countries is dwindling. By creating a border or an odd corner in which wildflowers can grow, the gardener is increasing the opportunity for these exquisite plants to continue.

Below
A variety of wildflowers creates a jumble of colors and shapes in contrast with the straight lines of the path.

Wildflower borders

Wildflowers can be added to a general border or they can be grown in a separate border devoted to them alone. The main problem involved in mixing them with other plants is that wildflowers are not always very colorful. They frequently have a delicate, understated quality and if they are mixed with more showy cultivated plants, they tend to get lost. The other major disadvantage with a mixed border is that the survival of wildflowers often depends on their being able to self-sow freely, and this can be a nuisance if they are grown with other plants that have a more fixed position in the border.

A border devoted to wildflowers is more satisfactory as long as you do not expect it to be too regimented or overwhelmingly beautiful. Although all garden species started as wild plants, many have been selected and bred for size and color until they are far removed from their wild counterparts.

Natural setting

The best way with wildflowers is to try to put them in their natural setting. They not only look better but grow more happily. Thus meadow plants should be grown with other such plants, along with grass; woodland plants should be grown under trees, and water plants inevitably should be grown beside water.

Wildflower meadows

The most popular way of growing wildflowers is in a meadow setting, from which many come. A wildflower meadow may seem like an impossibility in a small town garden, but there is no reason why one should not be easily made. Indeed, the basic requirement may well already be in place. This is the lawn. Choose part (or all) of the lawn and plant some wildflowers in it in the spring, and that is more or less it. Do not cut the grass until midsummer, by which time the flowers should have seeded to provide more flowers in the coming years. Cut it again at least once more before winter, then leave it until the following summer.

Alternatively, start from scratch with bare earth that has been completely cleared of perennial weeds. This is important as coarse weeds and grasses will quickly swamp the flowers. You want soft grasses instead. In spring, rake over the soil and sow a mixture of grass and wildflower seed and proceed as for a meadow made from a lawn.

Woodland borders

Of all plants used in a woodland border, unimproved woodlanders always seem to look best. The character of the habitat is so strong it needs something sympathetic to go with it. It is impossible to have a full-scale wood in a small garden, but one or two shrubs planted together can still create the same effect and form the perfect place to grow woodland wildflowers.

Odd corners

Wildflowers will colonize any odd space that is unoccupied. Normally such plants in a garden are called weeds. Indeed, they usually are coarse plants with little visual merit. Some are useful for other reasons: a colony of stinging

nettles (*Urtica dioica*), for example, is a good breeding ground for certain butterflies. There is no reason why the weeds cannot be replaced by other more attractive wildflowers. One good place to let them grow is along a hedge, where few cultivated plants will grow.

Acquiring wildflowers

Until recently the only way to acquire wildflowers was to take them from the wild, which rather defeated the point of conservation. Fortunately, this is no longer the case, as there are several seed companies that offer wildflower seed of a wide range of plants. They also sell mixtures, often tailor-made for the type of soil you have in your garden.

If you are planting into existing grass, it is usually easier to get wildflowers established by planting plants rather than scattering seed. Once these plants have established themselves, their own seed will eventually start to germinate and form a better meadow.

Below
Poppies (*Papaver*), phacelia, and other meadow annuals can be grown in any plot of disturbed ground.

Plants for wildflower meadows

Achillea millefolium Yarrow
A medium-height perennial with white flowers in summer

Ajuga reptans Bugle
A low-growing, spring-flowering perennial

Campanula rotundifolia Harebell
A low-growing perennial with blue flowers in summer

Cardamine pratensis Lady's smock
A small perennial with lilac flowers in spring

Centaurea scabiosa Knapweed
A medium-sized perennial with purple pincushion flowers in summer

Fritillaria meleagris Snake's head fritillary
A small bulb with red-purple flowers in spring

Geranium pratense Meadow cranesbill
A medium perennial with blue flowers in summer

Narcissus pseudonarcissus Wild daffodil
A small bulb producing yellow trumpet flowers in spring

Primula veris Cowslip
A low-growing perennial with yellow spring flowers

Prunella vulgaris Self-heal
A low-growing perennial with blue summer flowers

Ranunculus acris Meadow buttercup
A small summer-flowering perennial with bright yellow blooms

Stellaria graminea Chickweed
A low-growing perennial with white flowers in spring

Fragrant plants

Many people judge a border by the color of its flowers. However, there are many other qualities that go into making a good border, including foliage. One other quality that should not be forgotten is scent. Fragrant plants are often the making of a garden, the finishing touch.

Key to Planting

1	Osmanthus delavayi	6	Phlox paniculata 'Silver Salmon'	12	Dianthus 'Mrs. Sinkins'	18	Lonicera periclymenum 'Serotina'
2	Nicotiana sylvestris	7	Crambe cordifolia	13	Nepeta x faassenii	19	Jasminum officinale
3	Choisya ternata	8	Cestrum parqui	14	Lupinus 'Inverewe Red'	20	Rosa 'Climbing Etoile de Hollande'
4	Rosa 'Kathleen Hartop'	9	Lilium regale	15	Philadelphus 'Manteau d'Hermine'		
5	Daphne x burkwoodii	10	Anthemis 'Powis Castle'	16	Lavandula angustifolia		
		11	Petunia (blue variety)	17	Rosa 'Leverkusen'		

Fragrant flowers

The most evident smells come from the flowers. Not every plant has fragrant flowers but a surprising number do. They vary between those that give off enough fragrance to perfume the whole garden to those that have a delicate smell that almost requires the nose to be placed right inside the flower. Some have a curious scent that perfumes the air around but cannot be smelled up close.

The temperature and the time of day also affect scent; most flowers only smell if the air is warm, and they need a sunny day before they can perform. Others smell only in the evening or at night. This is because they are trying to attract night-flying pollinators such as moths. Include such plants in a border near where you sit outside in the evening to relax or entertain.

There are fragrant flowers for all times of the year. There is a surprising number of fragrant winter-flowering plants, probably because their fragrance ensures that they attract the limited number of pollinators that are around at that time of year.

Fragrant foliage

As well as flowers, the foliage of many plants is fragrant. In a few cases the scent is all-pervading, but generally the leaves need to be crushed or brushed before the scent is released. In even fewer cases there has to be some other stimulus; some plants are fragrant only after rain, while others need to be hot.

It is sensible to position the plants that need to be crushed before the scent is released alongside a path, so that you can run your fingers through them as you pass. Even brushing clothes is enough in many cases to envelop the passerby in scent. If the plants are planted farther back in the border, they cannot be reached easily, and an opportunity is missed. Those that require rain or a moist air to release their scent, such as the eglantine rose (*Rosa rubiginosa*), can be planted farther back. Many plants have foliage that is fragrant at all times of the year, and these are especially valuable.

Evil smells

Not all perfumes emitted by plants are pleasant. Some, such as that of dracunculus, are positively evil. These fetid smells usually come from plants that are pollinated by flies, attracted to the smell of rotting flesh. Attractive as many of these plants are, they are not ones to be planted in borders close to the house or places where you sit and relax. Other plants, such as *Lilium pyrenaicum* and *Phuopsis stylosa*, have a foxy smell most people hate, although a few actually find the smell appealing. Again, be careful where you site such plants.

Capturing the smells

Smells are very ephemeral, but it is possible to capture the smell of a border by making a potpourri of some of the plants. This is not difficult as long as you remember to pick the flowers while they are young. The fragrance of herbs can be kept by drying them in bunches.

Below

Some plants, such as this sage, *Salvia officinalis* 'Tricolor,' only release their scent when the foliage is touched.

Fragrant flowers

Choisya ternata Mexican orange blossom
A medium shrub with white flowers in summer

Convallaria majalis Lily of the Valley
A low-growing perennial with white flowers in late spring and early summer

Crambe cordifolia
A rosette-forming perennial with a huge spray of white flowers in summer

Daphne tangutica
A medium shrub with pink summer flowers

Dianthus 'Mrs. Sinkins' Pink
A low-growing perennial with white flowers in summer

Hesperis matronalis
A short-lived perennial with white or purple flowers in summer

Lilium regale Lily
Tall bulbs with glorious white trumpet flowers in summer

Lupinus Russell hybrids
A medium perennial with spikes of pepper-scented flowers in summer

Mahonia x media Charity
A medium to large shrub with yellow flowers in winter

Philadelphus 'Manteau d'Hermine' Mock orange
A low-growing shrub with white summer flowers

Rhododendron luteum
A medium-sized azalea with yellow flowers in summer

Sarcococca confusa
A low-growing shrub with white winter flowers

Syringa vulgaris Lilac
A medium-large shrub with white or lilac flowers in summer

Fragrant foliage

Aloysia triphylla Lemon balm
A frost-tender, low-growing shrub with lemon-scented foliage

Cistus purpureus
A medium-sized, bushy shrub with exotic flowers and a sharp, aromatic scent

Geranium macrorrhizum
A low-growing perennial with pink flowers and a strange, citrus scent

Laurus nobilis Bay
A medium-to-tall shrub with glossy evergreen foliage and a mellow savoury scent

Lavandula angustifolia Lavender
A small shrub with purple-blue flowers and a well-known fragrance

Myrtus communis Myrtle
A medium-to-large, dense shrub with fragrant white flowers and aromatic foliage

Perovskia atriplicifolia
A medium-sized subshrub with blue flowers and a sharp musky scent

Rosa rubiginosa Eglantine
A medium-sized rose with pink flowers and apple-scented foliage

Rosmarinus officinalis Rosemary
A medium-sized shrub with spiked, strongly aromatic foliage

Salvia officinalis Sage
A small-to-medium, evergreen shrub with a musky scent

Santolina chamaecyparissus Cotton lavender
A small-to-medium shrub with silver foliage and a strong sharp fragrance

Thymus vulgaris Thyme
A low-growing, bushy shrub with a mellow savory scent

Grasses

The beauty of grasses in the garden has been much more appreciated of late, and because of this, many more species and cultivars are now available through nurseries and garden centers. They can be used in a separate border devoted just to grasses or mixed in with other plants. Either way, they are plants well worth considering.

Below
There is a wide variety of grasses that can be used to create dramatic and exciting borders.

The beauty of grasses

Grasses have a beauty and elegance that it is difficult to find in other plants. This is mainly because of their thin stems, which not only make the plants graceful but allow them to move so beautifully in the wind. Not all grasses do this as some are low and form dense mats or tussocks. These depend on their color and texture for their impact. The flowers, which do not look like flowers in the conventional sense, are also a large part of the beauty. In some grasses they play little part as it is really the foliage that is important, but in others these silky heads create a great impact.

A grass border

It is possible to have a border devoted entirely to grasses. The arrangement is less dependent on color as the majority are green, although there are number that have very attractive colored foliage, including variegated. The arrangement has more to do with size, shape and texture. Unlike conventional borders, the effect also has to do with movement. The tall grasses in particular move with the slightest breeze. They sway gracefully and the plumes of flowers may look like streamers. With this movement comes sound: the rustling of the stiff leaves as they rub against each other. This can be a very soothing and restful sound.

One of the problems with a grass border is that all the plants seem to be at the same stage at the same time. In the spring there is little to look at as the majority have been cut back to the ground. A few, stipa for example, grow and flower by early summer, but the majority take longer. Comes the autumn and they are turning brown. Fortunately, this last stage is attractive in many species, and the dead stems can be left throughout the winter as part of the border's lasting attraction.

Above
Ornamental grasses can be used to dramatic effect to provide a contrast of shapes and textures among more conventional plants.

Grasses in a mixed border

Unless you intend to collect grasses, it is better to mix them in with other plants, especially in a small garden where space is limited. The grasses often add something to the border that other plants cannot. This is particularly true of the tall grasses such as the miscanthus, which produce a tall green fountain of stems and narrow foliage, topped with silky tassels of flowers. The shape is impressive in its own right, but it becomes even more so when contrasted with other plants in the border.

Smaller grasses also have their place, especially the ones with silky heads, such as pennisetum, which just invite you to stroke them. The low, lumpy ones, that depend more on their foliage color, are more difficult to accommodate as they often look lost among herbaceous plants.

Bamboos and sedges

Bamboos are similar to grasses and can be used in the same way. However, many of the bamboos run rather vigorously and are not really suitable for adding to a mixed border as they are difficult to control. They are better used as single plants, in borders that are allowed to run wild, in special borders devoted to them or in containers. They have the advantage that they do not die back in the winter and can also be relied upon to create a wonderful rustling sound in the breeze.

Sedges are another close ally of the grasses. They have the advantage that many are evergreen. They are mainly grown for their foliage rather than their flowers. The leaves are often variegated. They make good front-of-border plants and many can be used in woodland and shade borders for which not many grasses are suitable.

Grasses for the border

***Alopecurus pratensis* 'Aureovariegatus'**
A medium grass with yellow-variegated foliage

Arundo donax
A huge plant with blue-green leaves

Briza media
A low-growing grass with green leaves and purple-brown flowers

***Cortaderia selloana* Pampas grass**
A tall clump-forming grass with white plumes

Elymus magellanicus
A low-growing, spreading grass with blue foliage

***Hakonechloa macra* 'Aureola'**
A medium grass with yellow-variegated leaves

***Milium effusum* 'Aureum'**
A low-growing, spreading grass with yellow-green foliage

Miscanthus sinensis
A tall stately grass with green foliage

Molinia caerulea
A medium-to-tall grass with green foliage and purple flower spikes

Pennisetum villosum
A medium grass with green foliage and fluffy white flower heads

Phalaris arundinacea* var. *picta
A small-to-medium, spreading grass with silver-variegated foliage

Stipa gigantea
A tall tuft-forming grass with oat-like flower heads

Theme Borders

With a limited number of plant suppliers in the neighborhood it is often difficult to see how to create borders that are different from your neighbors'. On the whole, of course, it comes down to how you use the plants, and somebody with skill can always make ordinary plants look special. However, creating special borders is also a good way. It may be that you are not particularly interested in one type of plant over another, but there are still things that can be done. One example is the theme border.

The theme border

The idea of a theme border is to bring together plants that have some common element. It may be a common physical characteristic such as a certain color or a type of plant, as already discussed. However, there are more interesting themes that can link with other interests. For example, you could create a border that just contained plants mentioned by Shakespeare or those that appear in the Bible. A more unique type of border would contain things with a personal connection of some kind, perhaps through a name.

Advantages of a theme border

Theme borders can be completely unique,and most visitors will be fascinated by them. The advantage for the gardener is that a theme gives them an aim. It extends gardening beyond simply working the soil and plants. Winter evenings can be spent searching through books and catalogues for plants to add to the collection. Browsing around unknown nurseries becomes more pleasurable as you search out new plants. In a way, the border is never finished; there is always something extra to add.

Name borders

One idea is to choose something personal, perhaps plants bearing your name or that of someone else in the family. For example, the name Julia crops up in quite a number of plants, such as *Aster novi-belgii* 'Julia' and *Calluna vulgaris* 'Julia'. If you want to extend the list, add in names that include Julia as part of the name, such as *Clematis* 'Madame Julia Correvon'. The names Ann, Anne, or Anna occur in hundreds of cultivars, and Margaret is not far behind. In many cases there are enough plants to make a complete border, whereas in some there are only a few and it would be best to mix them into a general border, adding to them as you find more.

Friends and neighbors

One of the great joys of gardening is the tremendous friendship that it engenders. Most gardeners are very generous and are always giving away and receiving plants from friends, and sometimes even strangers. So often you forget the name of the plant, but very rarely the person who gave it to you. "Mrs. Brown gave me that just before she died," "I grew that as a cutting from Ida's wedding bouquet." Such are the memories that go with so many plants. A border devoted to plants that you associate with friends is truly a unique border. It will also be one that will give you a great deal of pleasure.

Personal borders

There are many other personal borders that you can create. An anniversary border, filled with favorite golden flowers for a gold wedding or silver foliage for a silver wedding; a border of Himalayan plants to remind you of a holiday in that part of the world; or perhaps plants mentioned by a favorite author. The list is endless, mainly because it is dependent on individuals and their life and interests.

Right
A pair of Shakespeare borders composed of plants mentioned in his plays, including sweet cicely, thyme, and columbines.

The Flower Arranger's Border

The art of flower arranging has exponents at all levels. Some are content simply to take a few stems of one plant and place them in a vase, others need a wide range of flowers, stems and foliage before they can produce a display. Whatever the style of arrangement, the arranger needs flowers. They can be purchased, of course, but no florist has a wide enough range for personal choice, and that little something for the final touch is needed long after you have left the shop. One way of ensuring a plentiful supply of material is to devote a border to flowers and foliage for cutting.

Left
A general border in which many
of the plants can be used as
cutting material for flower
arrangements.

The general border

In the small garden where space is at a premium, there is rarely room for specialized borders. You are better off creating a general border that not only satisfies your need for an attractive garden, but also provides for your special interest. A surprising amount of flower material can be used as cut flowers as long as it is conditioned properly after cutting. Not all last as long as those traditionally accepted as cut flowers, but they will still often last happily for several days.

One of the disadvantages of using a general border for cut flowers is that you are always cutting material from it. This can leave holes in the display, especially if you need several stems of the same plant. The border can become a bit dull, full of cut-off stems. For example, the regal lilies planted in the center to be a focal point will leave a hole when you decide that they would look better in a vase. The other problem is that you are constantly trampling all over the border to reach the flowers. This can create compaction, which is not good for the soil in the border.

Above

Dahlias can be grown in a general border, or, more commonly, they can be grown just for cutting in a special border.

Flowers for cutting

Alchemilla mollis **Lady's mantle**
A low-growing perennial with frothy lime-green flowers

Alstroemeria aurea
A medium-height perennial with straight stems of orange flowers

Convallaria majalis **Lily of the Valley**
A low-growing perennial with scented white flowers

Dahlia 'Bishop of Llandaff'
A large bulb with stunning scarlet blooms

Dianthus 'Doris' **Pink**
A low-growing perennial with lots of little pink flowers

Gypsophila paniculata
A medium-height perennial with large sprays of tiny white flowers

Lathyrus odoratus **Sweet pea**
A climbing annual with scented flowers

Molucella laevis **Bells of Ireland**
A tall annual with spikes of green flowers

Narcissus 'Peeping Tom'
A miniature daffodil with endearing yellow flowers

Nigella damascena **Love in a mist**
A medium-height annual with soft blue flowers

Rosa 'Golden Wings'
A medium-to-tall rose with yellow flowers

Rudbeckia hirta
A medium-height perennial with huge golden daisy-like flowers with black centers

The cutting border

If you have the space, one way around this is to create a border especially for cutting material. This can be arranged as an attractive border but it is more likely to be arranged in rows so that there is easy access. Since most stems are required to be straight, plants can be more rigidly staked than they are in a general bed. Staking does not look very nice, but it serves its purpose and does not look so out of place in a cutting border. Another advantage is that plants can be grown in larger quantities. You can have a whole row of, say, chrysanthemums or dahlias, which if used in the same quantity in a general border would swamp it. Flowers for drying can also be grown in rows.

Prepare such a border in the usual way. The plants should be planted farther apart than in a general bed so that there is plenty of air and light around them, encouraging the stems to grow as straight and perfectly as possible. Plenty of space also allows you to check and control pests and diseases and any defects. Make certain that the plants are well staked, either individually or tied to wires. Keep the plants watered and feed them regularly. For larger flowers, remove some of the buds to encourage the others to fill out.

The exotic

With transport so readily available, many of the flowers in the florist's shop are exotic plants that have been flown in from all over the world. The gardener cannot hope to compete with this vast range, but there are still quite a number of plants that can be grown in a conservatory or greenhouse border. The beds will need to be kept sufficiently warm and humid, but there is quite a range of exotic plants that can be grown in small quantities.

Vegetables

Not all gardeners have space to grow enough vegetables to keep them going for the whole year, but many have room for just a few. There is a tremendous satisfaction in growing vegetables well. Another aspect that is often overlooked is that they make very attractive garden plants.

Why grow vegetables?

Flavor in vegetables depends partly on the variety and partly on the freshness. Most varieties found in supermarkets have been chosen for their appearance, their ability to travel without damage, and the fact that they can be harvested all at once. Flavor comes near the bottom of the list, if it is considered at all. Vegetables grown in the garden can be chosen from a long list of seeds, many of which have been bred for flavor. However, the most important thing is that homegrown vegetables can be taken from the garden to the kitchen and onto the table in a matter of minutes; no greengrocer can ever provide such fresh produce.

There was a time when garden vegetables were much cheaper than those bought at the store. This is still true if you only count the cost of the seed, but with the tendency to count the cost of time as well, they are much more expensive. But that discounts the pleasure the gardener gets from growing them and, of course, the superior flavor.

Traditional beds

Vegetables are generally grown in rows in rectangular plots. If well tended, with healthy plants and no weeds, this type of bed can be very attractive. There is not necessarily much color, but the rhythm of the rows and the varying textures and shapes of the plants create a very satisfying scene. Planting in rows makes the bed easy to attend to and harvest the plants, as well as allow air to freely circulate.

Right
Neat rows of carrots, onions, cabbages, and Brussels sprouts in a traditional vegetable garden.

Blocks and deep beds

Another way is to grow the plants in blocks instead of rows. This allows for areas of deeply cultivated soil that are never walked on. The extra fertility, good structure of the soil, and lack of paths between each row allows more plants to be grown in a smaller space. However, air does not circulate as well and although it should be possible to reach each part of the individual beds, it is not so easy to see or reach the bottom of individual plants. Planting in blocks is still, however, a good idea for the small garden.

Potagers

Potagers are, strictly speaking, kitchen gardens (from French, literally, a garden for soup vegetables), but they have taken on the meaning of decorative kitchen gardens. Here

the beds are laid out more like borders, divided by attractive groupings or patterns. Fruit trees are grown over arches along the paths, and beans are grown up tripods or pillars at key points. Flowers are often incorporated, especially those that have traditionally been grown in kitchen gardens, such as sweet peas and nasturtiums.

The whole thing is attractively laid out, yet at the same time it is productive. The only problem is that sometimes it looks so good that it seems a sin to pull out a lettuce or dig some leeks.

Mixing it up

In the traditional cottage garden, flowers and vegetables were often mixed together. There is no reason at all why this should not still be

done. Vegetables can be very attractive in their own right and can hold their own in a flower border. A tall pyramid of runner beans, for example, is attractive both in flower and fruit. Ruby chard with its brilliant red stems or carrots with their filmy foliage take a lot of beating as ornamental plants.

Below

The formal lines of box hedging provide a note of restraint to the riot of vegetables in this spectacular potager.

Herbs

Although relatively few herbs are used today, herb gardens still have a great romantic appeal. However, a full-scale herb garden requires a lot of space as well as upkeep, but an herb border is well within the means of most gardeners, even those with small gardens.

Romantic qualities

One of the joys of an herb garden is the softness of it. The flowers tend to be small and quietly colored; there is no brashness. They often have a hazy or misty quality about them. The foliage is also somehow subdued. To add to the qualities, the herb garden always seems at its best on hot sunny days, which not only subdue the colors further but engender a feeling of drowsiness that is enhanced by the sound of bees droning about their business. When creating an herb border, it is important to incorporate a seat either in or near it, so that the gardener and others can relax comfortably and enjoy it to the full.

Medicinal herbs

There is also the romantic notion that most people have about the use of herbs in the past. Many were associated with certain illnesses because of their appearance rather than because they actually cured them. Others did have curative effects but have long since been replaced by modern medicines. Yet others have never been replaced for some people and are now being rediscovered and incorporated into today's medicines. However, not many people maintain herb borders now for their medicinal value; indeed, without the detailed knowledge that our ancestors had of their plants, it can even be dangerous.

Culinary herbs

On the other hand, culinary herbs are still very much in use, although we probably use fewer now than in the past, and most people concentrate on only a handful of common ones, such as mint, parsley, and chives. But it is nice to have a wider range as every so often a recipe calls for something less common, something that the supermarket will not stock, such as fresh horseradish root. There is a wide range of herbs available as either seeds or plants, making it easy to create a well-stocked border at very little cost.

Siting the border

Most herbs need the sun and so it is best to site a border devoted to them in a sunny position. It should also be open so that plenty of air can circulate around and through the plants. The plants can in fact be incorporated into a more general border. Sage, rosemary, and lavender all make attractive border plants, while parsley, chives, and thyme are very useful for edging borders. However, placing them all in a single border is not only convenient for collecting them to use in the kitchen but creates its own atmosphere.

Designing an herb border

The important thing to remember about herb borders is the need for access. It is necessary to be able to get to all the plants to harvest them without trampling on other plants or compacting the soil. It could mean that the border is very narrow so that all parts can easily be reached or, more attractively, it could mean that a series of paths intersect the border. One popular design is to have a large circular or square border with paths radiating out from a central paved area.

It is important to remember the size that some of the herbs will attain. Sage, for example, will look the same size as parsley when you buy it in a pot but will soon spread and form a good-sized shrub. Do not plant such an herb in a narrow space or too close to its neighbors or it will soon swamp them.

Below
A box-edged bed in a ornamental herb garden is both beautiful and practical.

Borders by Style

It is possible to create a border or series of borders with no thought as to style, but it helps to have some idea of what you are trying to create. This will provide more satisfactory results and will save time and money if you suddenly realize you are moving in the wrong direction.

The style of your border is likely to reflect your lifestyle and general philosophy. A person with a neat and tidy disposition is more likely to go for a more formal style, with clear-cut lines. At the extreme, things might become minimal, perhaps in the Japanese style with gravel borders, a few boulders, and, say, a few grasses.

On the other hand, someone with a relaxed, even cluttered lifestyle may tend toward the informal. This could be a traditional cottage-garden border, with plants mixed in a riot of colors, shapes, and sizes, a border where plants are allowed to self-sow as they wish. Not all informal borders need be so unstructured, however; they can still be created with the sense of freedom, but with an overall design.

The style is likely to come from within, but influences are everywhere; there is no need to be bound by preconceived ideas. We are surrounded by images of gardens in books, magazines, and on television, so take advantage of these and make note of the things you like and the plants that will go with the style you want. Copy styles that you like, take photographs, and keep a notebook of ideas.

There are likely to be constraints on your choice of style. For example, you may want neat formal borders but have children who play football in the garden. A ball crashing through a cottage-garden border is less devastating than through a more formal one. The amount of time that you can spend in the garden is also a constraint.

Do not rush to put your ideas into practice, as mistakes can be costly. Envision the layout and mark out key points on the ground to see how it will work out. Try different arrangements. Spend time making lists of plants and draw them on roughly scaled plans to work out how many plants you will require. When satisfied, start collecting plants and laying out the border.

Formal Borders

A formal garden is more likely to appeal to those who are formal in other aspects of their lives, including the décor of their houses. They like clear, uncluttered lines and layouts with a certain amount of symmetry. However, such aesthetics need not be severe; there is a great deal of elegance and simplicity in such designs.

Straight lines

The formality of a formal border is partly defined by its shape and partly by its planting. The simplest outline is a straight line. Thus square and rectangular beds tend to be formal in shape. The longer the length of a line, the more formal it appears to be. Thus two very long straight borders disappearing into the distance with a path between them will have a very formal appearance. This can be spoiled by having plants flopping over the edge. The line must be clear cut and well defined.

Sinuous curves have an informality about them, but if the curve is continuous and forms a well-outlined circle or oval the formality is retained.

Tight control

An important aspect of formality is tight control of color and height of planting. There is often a uniformity about formality, especially in bedding schemes. Random heights or colors will spoil the controlled effect. For a formal effect, a number of the same plants should be used.

Symmetry and rhythm

Two other key factors in formality are symmetry and rhythm. If a border is divided into two or four parts and each part is planted with the same pattern of plants, then a formality is set up. The repeat of a pattern, or even an individual plant will set up a rhythm. This is most noticeable if

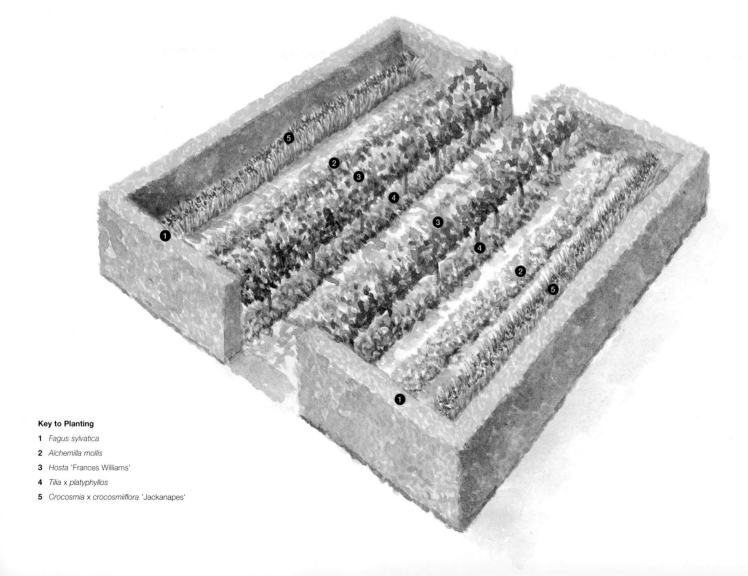

Key to Planting

1 *Fagus sylvatica*
2 *Alchemilla mollis*
3 *Hosta* 'Frances Williams'
4 *Tilia* x *platyphyllos*
5 *Crocosmia* x *crocosmiiflora* 'Jackanapes'

Above
A mixture of formality and informality.
The clear-cut edging of London pride,
Saxifraga x *urbium*, creates the
formality.

topiaried bushes are set at intervals down a long border.

Simple elegance

Formality can also be introduced by reducing the planting to a bare minimum with just a few simple shapes. This is often difficult to do in conventional borders with bare earth, but in a gravel garden, where the soil is covered in a raked layer of gravel, a perfect foil is created. Clumps of tall grasses, the rounded mounds of hostas, or the spiked, strap-like leaves of irises are perfect for such a border. It goes without saying that should weeds occur in such a border the effect is completely ruined.

Water

Water often associates well with this type of border. Not a natural pond, but a formal pond, fountain, or waterspout. The tinkling of falling water helps to create the effect.

Bedding

At the other extreme from simple gravel beds are tightly controlled formal bedding schemes. Once popular in the private garden, these have declined, but are now making a strong comeback. The plants are laid out in symmetrical patterns, often quite intricate ones. The overall effect is one of color and texture. Height is not so important, although each block or line of color is usually kept rigidly the same. The scheme may have taller plants in the center or at other key points.

Surroundings

It is difficult to create a single formal border when all around it is in chaos. It will only really work if all the borders are of the same style, at least in the immediate neighborhood. It is, however, perfectly possible to have a formal border that is enclosed within, say, a yew hedge with the rest of the garden in an informal style. The contrast then is all the greater and more effective.

Plants for balance and symmetry

Cordyline australis
A small-to-medium palm, perfect as a specimen plant

Cortaderia selloana Pampas grass
A tall grass forming a huge clump, good specimen plant

Dierama pulcherrimum Angel's fishing rod
A perennial forming a clump of grassy foliage with tall flower spikes, very architectural

Juniperus scopulorum 'Skyrocket'
A medium-tall conifer, forming an erect column

Laurus nobilis Bay
An evergreen shrub or tree, perfect for topiary and hedges

Lavandula angustifolia Lavender
A low-growing shrub, good for hedging and edging

Miscanthus sinensis
A tall architectural grass forming an upright clump

Rosa 'Fragrant Cloud'
A medium-height standard rose

Santolina pinnata subsp. *neapolitana*
A low-growing woody perennial, perfect for shaping and edging

Taxus baccata Yew
An evergreen tree or shrub, good for hedges and topiary

Yucca gloriosa
A medium perennial with a large rosette of stiff, sword-shaped leaves

Cottage-garden Borders

Most gardeners have a romantic notion about cottage gardens—they are brimming with flowers, everything grows extremely well, and nature takes care of all the problems. The reality is that a cottage-garden border involves as much hard work as any other type of gardening. However, the idea of it being full of color and ebullience is the essence of a good cottage garden, and there is plenty to be enjoyed.

Below
Even borders in a relatively formal garden can take on the informality of a cottage garden.

Informality

Probably the real key to the feel of a cottage border lies in its informality. Everything is packed in tightly with little regard to color, height and shape, and how they work together. The resulting riot of plants and color is the true glory of the cottage border.

These days it is impossible for any gardener not to be aware of at least some basic design rules and so we tend, perhaps, to be a bit more designerly than our ancestors would have been, but that is of little matter.

Control

Every garden needs some form of control, otherwise it will eventually return to a wild state, which inevitably means weeds and coarse shrubs such as brambles. The usual techniques of good preparation and weed and pest control must prevail. However, there are certain aspects about a cottage garden that do reduce the amount of work and attention required. The plants are set so close together that they act as a living mulch or ground cover and reduce the number of weeds that germinate. Planting close together and using strong plants means that

little time-consuming staking is necessary. The plants used are mainly old-fashioned varieties that have stood the test of time and have come down to us mainly because they are tough and not as prone to pests and disease as many of their modern counterparts.

Right
The hurly-burly of the cottage garden, where plants are crammed in a wonderfully informal way.

Plants

A wide variety of plants, including shrubs, perennials, and annuals, can be used. The annuals in the traditional cottage garden tended to be those that self-sow, rather than the modern types that need looking after before they are planted. These self-sowers were allowed to spread wherever they wished, which was part of the reason why the bed became a riot of uncontrolled color. The perennials and shrubs were those that are easy to look after. Little planning was done, and new plants, often arriving as a gift, would be inserted where there was a gap.

Later more control was introduced into such borders with the colors more organized, but the general feeling of informality and ebullience was retained. The modern gardener can choose which style to follow.

Vegetables

In the cottage garden, vegetables and flowers are often mixed. Even if they are not totally mixed, the vegetable patch merges with flowers and it is often difficult to tell where one starts and the other finishes. Many vegetables are decorative in their own right and can be used in the cottage border. Runner beans growing up tripods, for example, are good flowering, fruiting, and foliage plants and are good for providing height for the border. The only problem with using certain types of vegetables, such as lettuces, is that once they are harvested they leave a gap in the border.

Cottage-garden plants

Alcea rosea Hollyhock
A tall short-lived perennial with spikes of flowers in a range of colors

Aquilegia vulgaris Granny's bonnet
A medium perennial with blue-purple flowers in early summer

Campanula persicifolia
A medium perennial with blue, bell-shaped flowers in summer

Dianthus 'Mrs. Sinkins' Pink
A low-growing perennial with scented white flowers in summer

Fuchsia magellanica
A medium shrub with red flowers in summer and autumn

Lathyrus odoratus Sweet pea
A climbing annual with fragrant flowers in a variety of colors

Lavandula angustifolia Lavender
A low-growing shrub with lavender flowers in summer

Lonicera periclymenum Honeysuckle
A tall climber with scented, yellow-pink summer flowers

Lupinus Russell hybrids Lupin
A medium-height perennial with spikes of flowers in different colors in early summer

Primula vulgaris Primrose
A small perennial with yellow flowers in spring

Salvia officinalis Sage
A medium shrub with aromatic foliage and blue flowers in summer

Saponaria officinalis Soapwort
A medium-sized perennial with ragged pink flowers in summer

Parterres

Parterres and knot gardens are borders that are divided by low hedges. The patterns that these hedges make vary from the simple to the complex, sometimes with straight lines, sometimes with intricate curly patterns. Although these are often seen on a large scale in front of big houses, there are also many that have been constructed in small gardens.

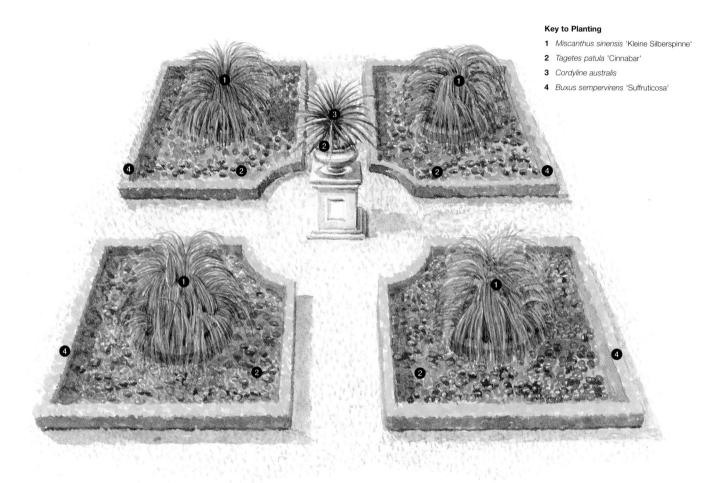

Key to Planting

1 *Miscanthus sinensis* 'Kleine Silberspinne'

2 *Tagetes patula* 'Cinnabar'

3 *Cordyline australis*

4 *Buxus sempervirens* 'Suffruticosa'

Hedges

The hedges used in parterres are relatively low, varying from about 12 to 18 inches (30–45 cm). Any taller than this and it becomes difficult to see what lies inside. The best material to use is box (*Buxus sempervirens*). This forms a dense, slow-growing hedge that keeps its shape and needs little trimming. Other suitable materials that can be used include santolina and teucrium.

Shapes

There is a wide variety of shapes from which to choose. For the small garden, a more simple arrangement would be best, possibly one based on straight lines and simple curves. In a larger garden there may be space to create a more complex pattern with paisley-like leaf shapes. Ideally, it should be possible to look at and appreciate the overall design of the parterre from ground level. In some cases, however, it may be necessary to look down on the parterre from an upstairs window or from a terrace to appreciate it fully, especially with the more complex designs.

The border need not be one solid shape broken up by hedges; it can also have paths running through it. Indeed, in the more simple cases, it is the paths that dictate the shapes while the hedges simply border these.

Source of designs

There are plenty of parterres illustrated in books, which will give ideas as to what can be achieved; herb gardens are often constructed in this way. Visiting gardens in which they are located is even better. There are other less obvious sources of inspiration. Books of designs and patterns will often give ideas. An even less obvious source might be books on patchwork quilts.

Infills

The areas within the hedges are as important as the hedges themselves. One traditional infill is colored gravel. The colors, often bright, vary from section to section, enhancing the pattern. However colorful this may be, plants are a better option for most gardeners.

There is a lot to be said for using plants with an even height and color. Annual bedding plants are perfect for this. They can be used in blocks, or each section can have plants in a mixed arrangement (pink tulips and blue forget-me-nots are a classic example). Another alternative is to use more than one type of annual but lay them out in a pattern within each section. It is possible to fill the spaces all year-round: pansies in winter, then spring bedding followed by summer bedding.

Another attractive alternative is to plant the various sections with herbs. This rarely has the same controlled appearance as annuals, as the size and shape of the herbs vary. Avoid planting large herbs near the hedges as they may swamp them. Such an infill is best suited to a simple design with paths running through it so that all the herbs can be reached easily.

Herbaceous plants can also be used, although they are likely to create a less formal appearance as they may have different heights and shapes. However, it is still a very attractive way of constructing a perennial border.

Below

Neat low box hedges divide the planting areas in this garden in an imaginative pattern creating a parterre.

Vertical Borders

There is a tendency to think of borders simply as two-dimensional objects, yet even the lowest still has height added to it by the height of the plants. However, walls and fences offer the opportunity to really think in three dimensions. Walls can be clothed in climbers to make, in effect, a vertical border. A vertical border could be at the back of a conventional border or be a border in its own right.

Below

A wooden tripod, covered by a clematis, helps to create a point of vertical emphasis in the border.

Climbers

There are a number of climbers that can be used at the back of a border or solely on a wall or fence. Roses, honeysuckle, wisteria, jasmine, and clematis, are just a few. Most of these have species and cultivars that are scented, which is an added advantage, especially if they are allowed to climb up around windows that are opened frequently.

A few climbers will cling to walls without support, but most need a structure to which they can cling, or onto which they can be tied. Wooden trellising can be used for small areas, but this will look too overwhelming if overused. A much better way is to use galvanized wires stretched horizontally along the face of the wall and held in position by vine eyes set at 4 foot (1.2 m) intervals.

Wall shrubs

There are a great number of shrubs that are frequently grown against walls. This is partly because they look good against walls, but mainly because the plants need some form of protection. Plants are likely to be blown about by winds rebounding off the wall, so although they are capable of supporting themselves, it is a good idea to tie them to wires attached to the wall.

Choose the shrubs in the same way that you would for any border, taking color, texture, and shape into consideration. Those that flower early in the year can have later-flowering climbers, such as clematis, trained to grow through them to increase their period of interest.

Climbing plants

Akebia quinata
A large plant with purple flowers in spring

Campsis radicans
A very tall climber with orange flowers in summer

Clematis montana
A very large plant with a profusion of pink flowers in spring and early summer

Cobaea scandens
A large annual climber with exotic purple and white flowers

Eccremocarpus scaber
A medium climber with tubular red flowers in summer

Hedera helix Ivy
A tall evergreen climber with green or variegated foliage, and berries in winter

Humulus lupulus 'Aureus' Golden hop
A deciduous climber with golden foliage

Hydrangea anomala subsp. petiolaris
A large climbing hydrangea with white flowers in summer

Lathyrus odoratus Sweet pea
A small annual climber with scented flowers in a range of colors

Lonicera periclymenum Honeysuckle
A large climber with scented pink-yellow flowers

Rosa 'Madame Grégoire Staechelin'
A large climbing rose with pink flowers in early summer

Wisteria sinensis
A large climber with sprays of white or lilac flowers in summer

Window boxes

In small gardens where space is at a premium, walls can be used to grow plants in a different way. Containers, such as window boxes, can be attached to the walls and filled with a wide variety of plants. Bedding plants, such as pelargoniums, will make a very colorful splash, but more sober perennials can also be used, including foliage plants, such as hostas, which are good for growing in shady areas. Wall containers can also be used for growing trailing plants like ivy. With imagination, a wall can be turned into a very varied and interesting vertical border.

Pergolas, arbors, and arches

Vertical emphasis is also important away from walls and fences. In the middle of borders,

Above

A simple rustic pergola covered in climbers creates a fragrant border through which you can walk

climbing plants can be used to climb over pillars and pyramids. Alongside borders, pergolas and arches can break up the flatness of the garden and create interest as well as cool areas through which to walk. Arbors can also be constructed to provide areas in which to sit and relax. These can be anywhere in the garden, but are enhanced when associated with a border. A path through a border leading to an arbor, perhaps covered in scented climbers, can be of great benefit. Such structures can be purchased from a garden center or can be made at home from rustic poles.

Island beds

Island beds, as the name implies, are beds that are surrounded by lawn or paths. They can be walked around and seen from all sides. They can vary from only a few feet across to beds where it is impossible to see from one side to the other because of the mass of vegetation they contain.

In the middle

The biggest advantage of island beds is that they utilize space in the middle of gardens that would otherwise be left empty. If all beds had a backing hedge, fence or wall, then they would all be strung out around the edges of the garden with nothing but a hole, usually left as a lawn, in the middle. An island bed not only makes this space more interesting but it also visually obscures some of the other beds so that the whole garden cannot be taken in at one glance.

Over the top

On the other hand, the biggest disadvantage is that if the bed is small, there is a great tendency to look either straight over the top of the bed or straight through the sparse vegetation to what lies beyond. There is no stop for the eye and however interesting the plants, the eye always seems to miss the bed in the middle. The only way to prevent this is by having tall, solid plants in the center.

Annual beds

The best use for island beds in many ways is for annual bedding. Here the display is very much for decoration and not for the appreciation of individual plants. It does not matter if the eye passes over or through; indeed, they are usually better appreciated if they can be looked down upon so that the patterning and colors can be seen. Generally the planting is low and may be repeated in several beds. The shapes of these beds are usually square, rectangular, or circular.

Below
A sinuous island bed with colorful planting that builds up to a peak.

Above

A small island bed raised
above the lawn to give it more
definition and interest.

Perennial and mixed beds

Perennials and shrubs create a different type of
island bed. Here the emphasis is more on the
plants than on their massed effect. The overall
effect is still important but not in the same
regimented way as with annuals. The problem
is scale. If the bed is too small the plants look
lost and get looked over in the same way as
annuals. Even if taller plants are used, the
colors and light will often penetrate through
them, creating an unclear and confusing
picture overall.

The advantage of conventional beds and
borders is that they have a backdrop that
frames the image and allows each component
to stand out. In order to achieve this with an
island bed, it should be quite large, so that it is
possible to have tall, solid material in the center,
which forms the backdrop, to the small and
medium-height plants that are positioned in
front of it.

The best island beds are so large that you are
unaware that they are islands. Here the center
can be built up with shrubs and even trees. The
shape in some ways is irrelevant as it cannot all
be seen at once. However, it must still make
sense. For an informal mixed border, a slowly
curving, sinuous line is often best. It can mirror
that of a bed on the other side of the path or
lawn. Always avoid sharp bends and corners
as these can look ugly and are difficult to plant
successfully.

Practicalities

With any gardening, the more skilled you are at the various techniques, the easier the task will be and the better the results. However, the "green thumb" myth need not worry beginners. Some people learn better than others, but most people are capable of learning the basic techniques. Indeed, these are so basic that many people acquire them without realizing it.

The simplest way to acquire skills is to get out there and try it. Very few things in gardening are irredeemable. Ruining some cuttings or snipping off the stem of an annual instead of a dead flower is not too serious, but losing expensive plants *is* costly so why not buy cheap ones until you have learned how to handle them? After all, most common plants are as attractive as the rarer (more expensive) ones—it is only their rarity that gives many such plants their appeal. Most plants are reasonably forgiving, and if you have put them in the wrong place, you can usually move them in the autumn or spring to somewhere more suitable. As long as you do nothing too drastic, nature will soon rectify a mispruning and give you another chance. The important thing is to learn from your mistakes.

Tools are a very personal thing. One gardener will love a particular type of hoe and could never be without it, while another gardener will hate it. Most modern tools tend to be the same size and weight. Try them in the store. If they do not feel right, try some second-hand ones instead. In the past there was a much greater variation in tools and many of them were made of very good quality steel. Go for the best tools that you can afford. Stainless steel is easier to clean but does not keep as sharp an edge as ordinary steel. Avoid gimmicks and go for a basic set of tools that you like and trust. Only hand tools are required for working borders; no machinery is required, except, perhaps, a shredder.

Most tasks are better done regularly rather than in sudden purges. A couple of hours a week is better than one day every four to six weeks. The garden will respond better and you will enjoy it more. Keeping on top of tasks is essential as nature is unrelenting. A new weed may take only a second to tweak out, but a month or so later it may take minutes or even hours.

Soil Structure and Conditioning

The soil is the single most important factor in any garden. It is vitally important that it should be thoroughly prepared, well maintained, and treated with respect. If the soil is looked after, then the chances of creating a great border are much enhanced. Ignore the soil, and it is likely to be an uphill battle.

Soil types

The best soil to have in your garden is a good loam. Few people, unless they are taking over an old garden, are likely to find this when they move in. However, it is possible to modify other types of soil so that you eventually come close to achieving it. Loam is a good, easily worked soil that consists of part clay, part sand and part organic material. Silty soils are a mixture of clay and sand. Improve them with organic matter.

Clay soils are heavy, stiff, and sticky. They are wet in winter and dry out and become like concrete in summer. They can be improved by adding plenty of well-rotted organic material and sand, which helps to break down the clay and improves drainage.

Sandy soils, on the other hand, are light and very free-draining. This quality is useful in moderation as plants hate growing in standing water, but excessive drainage means that there is no water for the plants. At the same time, any water that is added to the soil, either as rain or from a watering can or hose, has the annoying tendency of dissolving nutrients as it passes through the soil, taking them with it beyond the reach of plants. Because of this, a sandy soil is often a hungry one, as well as a thirsty one. Again, the addition of well-rotted organic material is the best solution.

Organic material

Organic material is vital to the soil, as it not only supplies a certain amount of nutrients but also holds enough moisture for the roots of the plants without leaving them soaking wet. There is a variety of materials that can be used.

Every garden should have a compost bin of some sort in which all waste garden plant material can be stacked to rot down. Apart from material containing weed seeds or pernicious perennial weeds, all garden waste can be composted, though some of the woodier material will have to be shredded first or it will take a long time to compost. Well-rotted garden compost is an excellent, and free, source of organic material.

Farmyard or horse manure is another good source. Even in urban areas it is often available from stables either within or on the outskirts of the town. This should be well rotted before it is added to the garden. When it is ready to use, it will be crumbly and free of smell. If poor quality hay has been used, however, farmyard manure can contain weed seed.

Another great source of organic material is leaf mold. No leaves should be burned; they should all be gathered up and added to the compost, or placed in a separate leaf mold bin to rot down. The results will be very valuable for use as a mulch and a soil conditioner.

Composted or chipped bark is not particularly valuable for adding directly to the soil, but is useful for top-dressing the borders. It will slowly rot down and then be added to the soil through natural action.

Adding the conditioners

When preparing a border, dig in as much organic material you can get. Once the bed has been planted, top-dress with material at least every spring and preferably every autumn as well. This will act as a mulch but will also gradually be incorporated into the soil to improve its quality.

Treat the soil with respect

Look after the soil. Regularly add organic material and, above all, do not work on it when it is wet. Doing so will compact it, ruining the drainage and breaking down its condition. If you have to work on wet soil, walk on a wide plank of wood to spread the load.

Left
A well-tended compost heap is a useful addition to any garden.

Right
A mixture of well-rotted compost and leaf mold makes the ideal material for conditioning and mulching borders.

Creating a Border

There are several stages in creating a successful border. The initial stage, the planning, can be carried out sitting indoors with only occasional trips outside to examine the site. The physical work starts with clearing the site, if necessary, and then digging it. Once this has been achieved, planting can begin as long as some thought and time has been given to acquiring the plants.

Drawing a Plan

Using squared paper, draw a rough plan to indicate the location and quantity of plants.

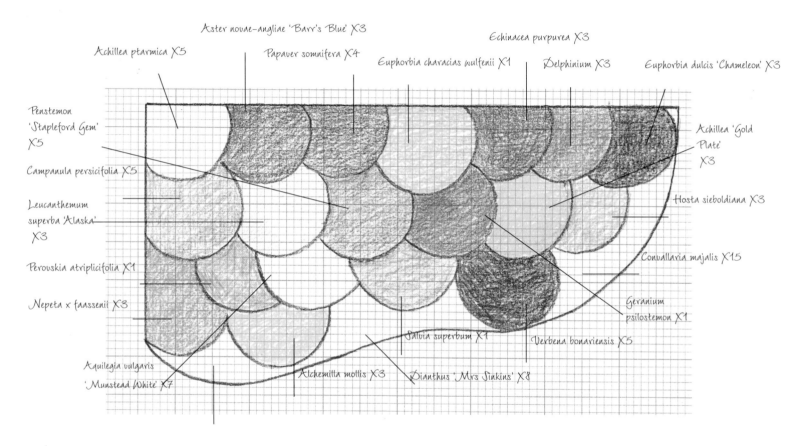

Aster novae-angliae 'Barr's Blue' X3

Echinacea purpurea X3

Achillea ptarmica X5

Papaver somnifera X4

Euphorbia characias wulfenii X1

Delphinium X3

Euphorbia dulcis 'Chameleon' X3

Penstemon 'Stapleford Gem' X5

Achillea 'Gold Plate' X3

Campanula persicifolia X5

Leucanthemum superba 'Alaska' X3

Hosta sieboldiana X3

Perouskia atriplicifolia X1

Convallaria majalis X15

Nepeta x faassenii X3

Geranium psilostemon X1

Salvia superbum X1

Verbena bonariensis X5

Aquilegia vulgaris 'Munstead White' X7

Alchemilla mollis X3

Dianthus 'Mrs Sinkins' X8

Planning

It is always a good idea to work out what you want to achieve before you go out and confront the empty bed. Work out what type of border you want and what plants you would like to have in it. Even if you are hopeless at drawing, it is still a useful exercise to draw out a rough sketch of what goes where and what goes next to what. This will give you some idea of what the border will look like and also the type and number of plants you will need.

Acquiring plants

It is never too early to start collecting the plants required. If you do not buy them when you see

them, they are bound not to be available when you want them. If you need large quantities of plants, then it is cheaper to propagate your own. This is best undertaken well in advance so the plants are mature enough to plant outside.

Keep the plants in a cold frame or even in a paved area that is defined by one or two rows of loose bricks. This will keep all the plants together and prevent them being blown or knocked over. Keep them watered and in the shade if they are woodland plants.

Outlining the border

If the border is a simple square or rectangle, it

can be easily measured out and marked on the ground using sticks and string. For squares and rectangles, check the length of the two diagonals, which should be the same if everything is square.

To mark out a simple circular border, insert a stick in the center of the proposed bed. Tie a string to the stick, the length of which should be half the width of the proposed circle (that is, its radius). Tie a narrow-necked bottle filled with sand to the other end and walk around the stick keeping the string taut and allowing the sand to trickle out of the bottle, thus marking the circle. An ellipse can be created using a similar technique. This time, use two sticks set some distance apart and a large loop of string. Place the string over the two sticks and walk around the outside, pulling the string taut and marking the edge of the border in the same way as before. Practice first, adjusting the length of the string and the distance between the sticks to get the shape of ellipse that you want.

More sinuous or complicated shapes can be worked out on the ground by laying down a hose and moving it around until the shape you want is found. Hoses tend to form smooth curves, so they are perfect for this task. Alternatively, plan the shape on paper and transfer it to the ground by drawing a grid of lines on the plan and then creating a similar grid out of canes and string on the ground. Use this grid as a guide to mark out the lines on the ground.

Preparing the border

Preparing the border is the most important thing you will do. Prepare it well and the gardening will be easy and the enjoyment great, prepare it badly and the border will become a chore. The first thing is to remove all perennial weeds. Make sure you dig up every bit of root as the plants will regrow if you leave any. If any remain when the border is planted they will be difficult

to remove and are likely to spread quickly into the plants, making them impossible to extract without taking the plant apart.

Dig the bed thoroughly, preferably in the autumn, adding as much organic material as you can. By the spring, the elements should have broken down the soil, and any bits of weed that remained should have reappeared. Remove these, and any annual weeds that have emerged, and rake the soil over to create a fine, level surface ready for planting.

Planting

Water all the plants about one hour before planting them to allow the compost in the pots to soak and become moist. Place the plants in their pots on the bed according to your plan or your inclination, stand back, and try to envision the plants in full growth. Readjust the spacing and layout if necessary. Then, starting at the back, plant the bed, setting each plant at the same depth as it was in its pot. Water all the plants thoroughly after planting. Rake the bed and apply a mulch of organic material to conserve moisture and further improve the soil structure when it is finally incorporated.

Above
When planting in an existing border take the opportunity to rejuvenate the area around the plant with organic material.

Below
Mark out the positions of different planting areas with a light-colored sand to see how they will fit together.

Building a Rock Garden

Borders for alpines and rock plants need special attention. These plants are often very delicate and should not be planted in a normal border or they will rapidly disappear. One of the ways of coping with them is to build a traditional rock garden. This is a border that incorporates blocks of stone and is designed in such as way that it resembles a piece of natural landscape or a rocky outcrop.

Right
Alpines thrive in raised beds
and are better positioned to
delight the eye.

Right
Alpines thrive in raised beds and are better positioned to delight the eye.

Appearance

The best rock gardens have such a natural feel about them that they could be a slice of mountainside. The grain of the rock is all laid in the same direction, and the blocks are all tilted back into the bed at the same angle, just as they would be in nature.

Choice of rock

There is a wide choice of available rock. The best is always that which is found in your locality as this will fit in naturally with the surrounding landscape. Hard granite in a sandstone area will immediately look out of place, for example. Local stone is also usually cheaper as it is the transportation that pushes the costs up. Use proper quarried stone and not that stolen from the countryside.

Always use proper rock. Avoid lumps of concrete and also the plastic rocks that have suddenly become available. The latter may look authentic, but rock plants need the cool root run and the moisture that they find under stones, and these fundamental requirements are completely lacking with their plastic counterparts.

The size of the stones should depend on what you are able to move. Large lumps will be too heavy to move without machinery. That said, it is surprising what can be moved using simple mechanical principles involving levers and rollers. However, moving rock can be very dangerous, and crushed fingers and back injuries can easily result.

Preparing the site

As with any border, make sure that you have removed all perennial weeds. Any that remain are likely to get into the stonework and

become impossible to remove without having to take the rockery apart to do so. Make certain that the site is drained. Even a pile of well-drained soil, which is essentially what a rock garden is, can easily soak up moisture from beneath and become saturated to the detriment of the plants.

The soil should be a good quality, free-draining loam. If you have a clay soil, it will pay to add some good topsoil. To one part of ordinary, reasonably draining garden soil, add two parts grit or gravel and one part of very well-rotted organic material such as leaf mold. Mix these together well.

Building the garden

Spread the first layer of soil mixture on the ground and embed the first row of stones into it so that they slope back gently into the rock garden. The stones should have at least one-third of their bulk below the soil level.

Build up the bed with more soil and add a second tier of stones, again embedding them well. Make certain that all stones are secure and do not rock. Add the third tier and so on until the garden is finished.

Planting

Set the plants into the pockets of soil between the rocks. Some plants, such as saxifrages, can be placed in narrow crevices between the rocks. In order to squeeze these in, wash the compost from their roots, wrap these in damp tissue, and then poke them into the crevices. Filter in some compost on top of the roots and then firm it in place if you can.

When all the plants are positioned, top-dress all the soil with a layer of grit or gravel. Gently push this under the leaves of the plants to protect them further.

Raised beds

Raised beds are also suitable places for growing alpines and rock plants. They are borders that are raised above ground level, with a low brick, concrete block, or wooden wall to hold the gritty, free-draining soil in place. The alpines are planted in raised beds in exactly the same way as in an ordinary border except that the surface of the soil is usually top-dressed with gravel after planting. Raised beds allow small alpines to be viewed and appreciated without them getting lost in larger borders.

Maintaining Borders

Borders need regular work to keep them in good working order and looking at their best. If
the border has been well prepared in the first place, the work should not be arduous; indeed,
many find it a pleasure to be working among the plants. The work is not difficult, especially
once you have begun to know your plants.

Weeds

Weeds and weeding are the two things that
seem to put many people off gardening.
There are, however, several ways in which
gardeners can reduce the weeding burden
to acceptable levels. The first of these is
very thorough ground preparation in which
all perennial weeds are removed.

The second is to tackle each of the borders
as early in the season as you can. If possible,
work in the winter as long as the weather and
soil conditions allow. This will mean that you
tackle any weeds left over from the previous

year before they start becoming a nuisance
and before the herbaceous plants get above the
ground, making it difficult to work. If you leave it
until the weather warms up, the weeds will be
ahead of you, and it is likely to become an uphill
battle, especially if you have several borders to
take care of.

Another way to reduce the amount of weeding
necessary is to apply a mulch of some form.
Do this after the winter or early spring weeding.
A deep layer of chipped bark or well-rotted
farmyard manure will prevent most of the
weeds from germinating.

It is never a good thing to use chemical weed-
killers in a border. Apart from any ethical
reasons that the gardener might have, it is
inevitable that the spray will drift or drop onto
plants as well as weeds, and a lot of accidental
damage can be done.

It is difficult to weed in a closely packed border
with a hoe. Such a tool is bound to accidentally
slice off the shoots of emerging herbaceous
plants, and it is difficult to see what you are
doing in densely planted areas. It is better to
weed by hand using a trowel or hand fork, or to
gently dig the bed with a border fork.

Right
A thick mulch of bark on a
border helps keep down weeds
and prevents loss of moisture.

Opposite
Supports are essential for some plants, but
they can look ugly unless they are used
discreetly.

Support

If you choose strong plants and place them
close together this may reduce the amount
of staking you have to do, but it also reduces
your choice of plants. Staking is essential to
prevent taller plants from flopping over, which
they may do because of weakness or damage
by strong winds. Rain can also make the
flowers, especially double blooms, very heavy
and bend the plants over.

Stake the plants before any such threats
appear. Do it when the plant is about half
grown and place the support at a level that will
be about two-thirds of the height of the mature
plant. In other words, you will be staking above
the plant. The plant will then grow up through
the supports. One way is to push pea sticks
into the ground and bend their tops over to
form a mesh of horizontal twigs. Another way is
place several short canes around the plant and

weave a cat's cradle of string between them.
The third way is to buy stakes. These come in
various forms, including bamboo, and metal
grids in the form of a circle. Single stems can
be supported by merely tying them to a cane
inserted into the soil.

Dying material

When flowers begin to fade, they should be
removed. This not only saves the plant energy
as it will not have to produce seed, but it will
also make the border look neater and allow the
remaining flowers to show up better. Some
plants can have their flower heads removed
after flowering is complete, while others can be
cut back to the ground so that new leaves can
come up to replace those that were beginning
to look old. Once the stems and leaves begin to
go brown, they too can be removed.

Vegetative versus seed

Vegetative propagation (taking part of the plant
such as a cutting or division, and rooting it)
has the big advantage that all resulting offspring
are identical to the parent plant. With seed,
however, this is not always true. Species and
some cultivars will be identical, but many of the
cultivars will produce offspring that differ from
them in size, habit, or color. So if you want to
be certain of reproducing a plant you already
own, it is safer to take cuttings rather than
seed. from the plant

Seed

Seed can be sown either in trays or pots, or
out in the open. For most practical purposes,
especially in a small garden, trays or pots
are best. Fill a tray or pot with a good seed
compost and sow the seed thinly on the top.
Cover this with a layer of 3/8 inch (4 mm) grit.

Increasing Plants

The ultimate challenge for many gardeners is to produce their own plants. There is something rather satisfying about starting with a tiny seed or a small piece of the plant and turning it into a thriving new plant. Although beginners will have a few failures, this should not make them despondent, as some plants are very difficult to increase even for experienced gardeners. However, the majority of plants are quite straightforward and should give no trouble, only pleasure.

Below
A well organized greenhouse shelf with plenty of young plants coming up.

Place the pot or tray in a shallow pan of water and allow the water to seep slowly through the drainage holes in the bottom of the pot to moisten the compost from below. Remove the pot when the gravel on top becomes moist.

Annuals will germinate faster if placed in a warm propagator, but perennials can be left on a greenhouse bench or placed outside in a sheltered spot. Once they have germinated, gently place the seedlings into individual pots or trays. Use a small stick or the tip of a pencil to help ease the roots of the seedlings out of the compost, handling the seedlings only by their seed leaves (the first pair of leaves that form). Replant them into individual pots or well spaced in trays of fresh compost in which to grow before planting out.

When the seedlings are large enough, harden them off to get ready for planting outside. This involves gradually introducing the plants to the conditions outside so that they do not get a shock when you plant them. Bring the plants out for just an hour or two a day at first, gradually increasing the length of time until they are staying out all day, and eventually all night. They will then be ready for planting outside.

Cuttings

Take stem cuttings of perennials and shrubs in midsummer. Remove the top 4 inches (10 cm) of nonflowering shoots to make cutting material. Cut the shoot down to 2–3 inches (5–8 cm), making the cut just below a leaf joint at the bottom of the cutting. Remove all the leaves from the stem except for the top pair.

Fill a 3 inch (8 cm) pot with cutting compost and tap on the table to settle the compost. Use a pencil to make holes in the compost around the edge of the pot, place the cuttings into the holes, then gently firm the compost back around the cuttings. Water and place in a propagator or plastic bag until the cuttings have produced roots. Place into individual pots and grow until large enough to be planted in the border.

Basal cuttings can be taken from some herbaceous plants in spring. Remove a few emerging shoots when they are 2 inches (5 cm) tall and treat as stem cuttings above.

Division

Many perennials can be divided to form a number of smaller plants, which will soon grow to the size of the parent. In fact, even if you do not want new plants, mature clumps of perennials actually benefit from being divided. As the old material in the center of the clump is discarded, the newer growth around the outside is rejuvenated.

First dig up the plant to be divided, then split the clump into a number of pieces. Large, coarse plants can be split most easily by inserting two garden forks, back to back, in the clump and levering them apart. Repeat this until the plant is broken down into small enough pieces, each with a portion of healthy top growth and some roots attached. Smaller and more delicate plants can be broken into pieces with the fingers.

Hold the plant in both hands and shake the earth off, gently working it with your fingers. Many plants, such as primulas, will then naturally fall into pieces. For plants that resist this treatment, try holding the plant in a bucket of water; as the soil is washed off, the individual crowns will part. Some plants are really tough, however, and it will be necessary to cut the clump into pieces, each with a growing bud and some roots.

However you divide the plant, discard any old material or pieces that look weak. The larger divisions can be planted back into the border, but the smaller ones should be potted in individual pots and kept in a cold frame for a few days before hardening them off. Once they are established in the pots, they are ready to plant outside.

Below
Taking cuttings is a simple means of increasing your existing plants. It is also usually cheaper than buying commercially grown plants.

Index

Page numbers in *italics* refer to illustrations.

Acknowledgements

Front cover: **Garden Picture Library**/Howard Rice.
Back cover centre and back flap: **John Glover**.
Back cover top left: **Octopus Publishing Group**.

Andrea Jones/Garden Exposures 49, 53, 80/Derek Harris 8–9, 22, 50/Designer: Robin Williams. Derek Harris 21.
Garden Picture Library/Linda Burgess 118/Juliet Greene 78–79/Jacqui Hurst 120.John Glover 4 Bottom Left, 5 Centre, 5 Bottom Right, 10, 12, 16, 27, 54, 66, 108/Designer: Chris Costin 18/Designer: Marnie Hall 75.
Harpur Garden Library 3, 36/Designer: Arabella Lennox-Boyd 14/Jerry Harpur 6–7, 88/Jerry Harpur 2/Marcus Harpur 89.
Andrew Lawson 4 Bottom Right, 11, 20, 26, 32, 33, 34, 55, 70, 82, 83, 87, 97, 109, 110–111, 112, 115 Top, 117/Hodges Barn, Gloucestershire 68–69/House of Pitmuies, Tayside 29/Designer: Wendy Lauderdale 43/Old Rectory, Sudborough, Northants 95.
S & O Mathews 35, 37, 38, 39, 40, 44–45, 48, 56–57, 58, 63, 98, 113.
Clive Nichols Photography Front and back endpapers, 4 Top Left, 31 /Bosvigo House, Truro, Cornwall 62/Designer: Mark Brown 91/Cambridge Botanic Garden 67/Chenies Manor, Bucks 47/Coton Manor, Northamptonshire 74/Designer: Wendy Lauderdale 24–25/Feibusch Garden, California 73/Hadspen Garden, Somerset 103/Heterton House, Northumberland 101/HMP Leyhill, Hampton Court 98 94/Designer: Wendy Lauderdale 76, 107/Lakemount, Cork, Eire 64/Leeds City Council, Chelsea 98 61/Designer: Leo Nederhof 85/Pam Schwert/S Kreutzberger 102/Sticky Wicket, Dorset 77/The Old Vicarage, Norfolk 30/The Old Vicarage/Norfolk 105/Designer: Julie Toll 84/West Green House, Hampshire 106/White Windows, Hampshire 71/Designer: Elisabeth Woodhouse 92.
Octopus Publishing Group Ltd. 4 Top Right.
Photos Horticultural 116, 119.
Rob Whitworth 17.
Jo Whitworth 23, 93, 96.